CALLED AS PARTNERS IN CHRIST'S SERVICE

Called as Partners
in Christ's Service

The Practice of God's Mission

SHERRON KAY GEORGE

Geneva Press
Louisville, Kentucky

Book design by Sharon Adams
Cover design by Night & Day Design

First edition
Published by Geneva Press
Louisville, Kentucky

This book is printed on acid-free paper that meets the American National Standards Institute Z39.48 standard. ♾

PRINTED IN THE UNITED STATES OF AMERICA

06 07 08 09 10 11 12 13 — 10 9 8 7 6 5 4 3 2

Library of Congress Cataloging-in-Publication Data

George, Sherron Kay.

    Called as partners in Christ's service : the practice of God's mission / Sherron Kay George.—1st ed.
      p. cm.
    Includes bibliographical references.
    ISBN-13: 978-0-664-50262-1 (alk. paper)
    ISBN-10: 0-664-50262-8 (alk. paper)
      1. Presbyterian Church (U.S.A.)—Missions. 2. Missions—Theory. I. Title.

BV2570.G46 2004
266'.5137—dc22

                                    2004041159

Contents

Foreword

A Foundational Memory

*M*y earliest memory of being involved in mission is a nighttime meeting held in a village room in the Punjab, India. My family was visiting my Uncle Ernie Campbell's family. Both families were Presbyterian missionaries, gathered together for Christmas. My uncle had been involved in flood relief in Punjab, and he had received word of a gift of money from a church in the United States to help local churches provide flood recovery aid to their villages. He invited my father to come along to a meeting of the elders gathered from a group of village churches. I also got to go at the tender age of six or so, and can only assume it was because I had been so tiresome my mother had sent me out with my father.

I remember getting to the village half-asleep, being welcomed with great joy and very hot, sweet tea. After the requisite conversation, the elders and my father and uncle gathered in a circle, sitting on the ground. I was relegated to a place along the wall with a warning to sit still and be quiet or else! The meeting began with prayer and words of greeting and my uncle's explanation that churches in the United States had sent a gift to help their churches assist their villages in recovering from the flood. My uncle asked the elders to tell him how the gift should be used. The oldest elder expressed gratitude for the gift and the solidarity it represented and told my uncle they would trust him to tell them how to use it. My uncle demurred and said that they were the ones who had the knowledge and they were the church in this place. The gift was for their use and they must decide.

There was silence while the host elder went through the lighting of the hookah (water pipe). Once this was lit, the oldest elder passed it to the first person in the circle and asked for his advice. The first person took a pull on the hookah as he thought and then spoke. After he spoke, he handed the hookah to the next person. That person took a pull on the hookah, expressed gratitude for the wisdom of the first speaker and then gave his opinion. So it went around the circle. I watched carefully because while my uncle was a smoker, my father was quite opposed to smoking. Yet to my amazement when the hookah came to him he also took a deep pull on it. He tried to excuse himself from giving an opinion, but the elder would not permit that, so my father gave thanks for the wisdom already expressed and then offered some thoughts of his own. After my uncle and all the rest of the circle had spoken, the old elder received the pipe back and smoked for some moments in silence. Then, thanking all for their wisdom, he offered his understanding of a plan that incorporated all the voices. With some minor revisions, their plan was adopted.

While still too young to know it, I was witnessing the best of mission in partnership. What made it work were not just the disciplines of mutuality and solidarity practiced, but deeply engrained attitudes that made the work done a common expression of response to God's call. It was representative, consultative, transparent, accountable, indigenously led, expressive of solidarity, and incarnational.

Historic Emphasis

While we tend to think of mission in partnership as a relatively new development, one of the first U.S. Presbyterian involvements in international mission came as long ago as the mid 1800s, when we joined with the Nestorian Church in Iran to extend the gospel to those who had not yet received it. Working with church partners has been important in many places. Where there was no church yet, we worked hard to develop an indigenous church with which to partner.

Root Meaning

My favorite understanding of the meaning of partnership comes from its base root in the English language. In its original meaning the word "partner" denoted not people who joined together in an enterprise but people who were joined together through the gift of a common inheritance. As Christians, we understand ourselves to be inheritors of God's gift of grace in Jesus Christ. In this, God makes us partners with everyone else in whom that grace is operative, and because it is the same grace, we are all equal in God's eyes and heart, despite what we might mistakenly think because of unequal distributions of wealth and power and geographic accident.

Theological Paths Lead to Partnership

Whether we approach mission theologically, ecclesiologically, pneumeno-logically, or developmentally, all lead to mission in *partnership*. As Sherron George will make clear to us, the very nature of God in our Christian Trinitarian theology requires the logic of partnership. The nature of the Ecclesia, the Church, is in its deepest sense the body of Christ. In this each denomination and congregation within it is a fractal, in itself incomplete but part of the fullness of what God intends the Church to be. To be that fullness that God intends, we need to be the Church and work as the Church together. The PC(USA)'s *Book of Order* puts it this way:

> There is one Church . . . while divisions into different denominations do not destroy this unity, they do obscure it for both the Church and the world. The Presbyterian Church (U.S.A.), affirming its historical continuity with the whole Church of Jesus Christ, is committed to the reduction of that obscurity and is willing to seek and maintain communion and community with all other branches of the one, catholic church.[1]

As one church, our respect for the sovereign initiative and mystery of God's will working through the power of the Holy Spirit leads us to a humility concerning our own involvement and to an appreciation of our need for others. Furthermore, the dynamics of our practical disciplines of development work have taught us that, for mission to have transforming effect, it must be participatory in design and implementation.

Biblical Grounding

Out of many possible biblical texts, Sherron George leads us through a compelling study of the Gospel of John. In this study we see there is a dance of divine movement, poetically introduced through the prologue of John (1:1–18), and developed and reinforced throughout the Gospel. In the study, we see that God chooses to be and to act in mission in ways that are always invitational, empowering, and relational and that God invites us to join the dance in mutuality with God and with one another. The language and power of that dance is ultimately the power of God's love, and Sherron teaches us that love is the heart of all mission in partnership.

Need for Definition

In the Presbyterian Church (U.S.A.) we have worked towards mission in partnership for many decades. We have, however, not found it easy to define or put into practice. Its rewards are great, but it calls us to careful steps in the middle of complex issues in which our realities enter as a third dimension into the lives of other people. We have worked for five years to define and redefine our "Presbyterians Do Mission in Partnership" policy. We sought to do that work by practicing the consultative partnership we advocated. We are satisfied that the current policy moves us forward even though it will continue to need refinement and care in implementation.

Attitudes, Not Regulations

One of our mission personnel who is not a U.S. citizen pointed out a weakness implicit in our title: "Presbyterians DO Mission in Partnership." I often feel that part of the genius of the United States is that we are all at some level engineers. To see a need makes us want to move to action. There is a gift in that, as we tend to get things done and develop good systems to keep action going. The downside is that we tend to reduce some issues to "resolvable problems" without fully understanding them and without thinking about how such issues may call for a different way of *being* rather than a different way of *doing*. I think this mission person was correct. Mission is not just about doing—it is also about *being*. Any motto invites errors of oversimplification and this one does as well, to mission is not just about doing, it is also about being. The question for us is not just what God is doing in the world, but how God is choosing to be present in the world. For us, it is about attitudes and understandings and theological beliefs and "the world's deep hungers and the deep gladness of our callings from God."[2] All of this is necessary if our "doing" is to have integrity.

In Part 2 of this book, Sherron helps us explore the attitudes necessary for our participation in God's mission to have integrity and to be healthy. For her those attitudes are respect, compassion, and humility.

Need for Care

We look for simple answers yet this is a complex world with countervailing forces and contradictory unintended consequences. We also are not neutral but carry in our identity considerable cultural and personal baggage. Our actions can cause significant impact on others—both Christian and non-Christian—in ways they may experience as harmful. The "Do No Harm" of the Hippocratic medical oath becomes a good approach for the care needed in mission work. History is replete with stories of the good and often unintended harm of mission endeavor. Given that long and conflicted history, why would a Christian not want his or her participation in mission to be checked and balanced by the larger community of the church? Partnership is in part the discipline of subjecting what we do in mission to the review of others—especially those most directly impacted.

This complexity and need for care leads to an assertion some have found difficult: that partnership is, and requires, a discipline. Not everything we think to do may be helpful. This discipline, like any art form, requires craft and practice. In her book, Sherron George calls us to two sets of practices: "Observing and Participating" and "Receiving and Giving."

Increasing Direct Missionary Involvement

In today's global world we see broadening opportunity for direct involvement in international mission. This can bestow great blessing as involvement in mission transforms individuals, their congregations, and the mission structures of our church and of our partner churches. It also presents inherent dangers as differences of wealth, power, worldview, and cultural awareness vary widely among those who seek to do God's work. Direct congregational or personal mission efforts sometimes bypass, or miss, the guidance of the church as God has created it in other places as well as the hard-won learnings that have come out of previous mission involvement.

Yet the call to mission is not optional for Christians. It is mandated. In the Worldwide Ministries Division of the PC(USA) we seek to support responsible direct mission with the creation of Mission Network tables, around which all Presbyterians engaged in mission in a particular place or cause can gather, learn, and seek God's guidance. We have also created a new type of mission service through the work of regional liaisons. A large part of each liaison's job is to serve as an informed resource for congregations and presbyteries in their direct mission work. (Sherron George presently serves in this capacity for us in South America.)

We are excited about this trend despite its complications. We see that as we enter into mission, whether through the mission work of a congregation, presbytery, or agency, we are transformed! We become different people. Our eyes are opened to new realities. . . .

All this leads to need for Sherron George's book. We are grateful for her writing it as a part of her mission service.

WILL BROWNE
Associate Director for Ecumenical Partnership,
Worldwide Ministries Division,
Presbyterian Church (U.S.A.)

Preface

*M*y pilgrimage toward partnership in mission began the day I arrived in Brazil in 1972 as a young adult mission worker under appointment of the Presbyterian Board of World Missions. Through a process of trial and many errors, in the context of the open and gracious Latin American culture, I discovered a new paradigm of mutuality and new attitudes and practices for mission. I give details of my transformational adventure in my essay "From Missionary to Missiologist at the Margins: Three Decades of Transforming Mission" in *Teaching Mission in a Global Context.* I think we have been suffering the birth pains of a new model of mutual partnership in Brazil and around the world for over half a century, but our practice continues to lag behind our rhetoric.

In my early ingenuous days I assumed that all mission relationships were loving, two-way partnerships based on respect—relationships that valued the gifts and dignity of all partners. I never imaged missionaries creating dependencies or humiliating anyone. Later I realized that unless we humbly, intentionally, and patiently build dialogical relationships and practice two-way mission *with* people, our cultural default is a demeaning one-way mission *for* people. I gradually learned that our way of being and our missional attitudes toward other people, religions, and cultures are more important than anything we can build, teach, or give.

I first worked in rural congregations in southwest Brazil as a Christian education consultant and then in north Brazil in Manaus as consultant and professor of mission and Christian education. In 1986 the Independent Presbyterian Church of Brazil (IPIB) invited me to teach mission at their seminary in Londrina. There students and professors challenged me both as a citizen of the richest country in the world and as a missionary from a dominating culture of rampant individualism. As I read and listened to Latin American theologians, bit by bit my own theology and missiology were turned upside-down. I was caught up in a process of continuing conversion and radical trans-formation. I was a participant observer of my students and colleagues as they reflected critically on North American mission and church and contextually analyzed Brazilian church and society. We became partners in teaching and learning. As the first ordained woman most of them had known, I stood in spe-cial solidarity with our female students, striving for the day when the IPIB would vote for the ordination of women, which happened in 1999. Later I con-tinued my journey by teaching at the seminary of the Presbyterian Church of Brazil (IPB) in Campinas.

After receiving much and giving what I could for twenty-three years—writing four books in Portuguese as a joint venture with my students, speak-ing and preaching, and serving as professor at several institutions—in the midst of fruitful activity I sensed God calling me in 1995 to return to the United States.

From 1996 to 2001 I had the privilege of teaching evangelism and mission at Austin Presbyterian Theological Seminary in Texas. The faculty and stu-dents helped me to relearn and reconnect with U.S. culture and church. I enthusiastically engaged in encouraging and equipping Christians in the United States to join God's mission near and far in the new millennium in a changed and changing culture, society, world, and church. I bonded with sig-nificant new conversation partners in the American Society of Missiology.

However, immersion in Brazilian culture had a greater impact on me than I realized. My transformation into a bicultural person at the margins had occurred. I am an ecumenical Christian, a member of the global faith com-munity who is passionately committed to God's mission. After a wonderful experience of teaching mission at Austin Seminary for five years, my love for Latin America and my desire to serve Worldwide Ministries Division (WMD) led me to be commissioned again as a PC(USA) mission coworker in 2001. I reside in Campinas, Brazil, serving as liaison and theological education con-sultant for South America and missiological consultant for WMD, a "feet-on-the-ground" missiologist missionary.

One of my first tasks as missiological consultant has been to help unpack the new policy statement "Presbyterians Do Mission in Partnership." The idea for this book emerged in my conversation with Peter Barnes-Davies, mis-sionary-in-residence, assigned by the Ecumenical Partnership Office of Worldwide Ministries Division to prepare resources to equip congregations to implement the policy. I presented to Peter my idea for the three parts of the book, one on theological foundations of partnership in the Fourth Gospel, a second on missional attitudes, and a final part on dyads of missional practices.

I shared my lists of attitudes and practices, and we began to brainstorm. From that moment, we worked closely and constantly together, Peter in Louisville and I in Brazil. I want to thank Peter for all his creative ideas, for his meticulous reading of the manuscript, for his many insightful suggestions, for struggling with me over titles and subtitles, and for his partnership every step of the way. He was the point person in negotiations with Geneva Press, including our initial conversation with editor David Dobson when we designed the basic format of the book. Peter did not leave me orphan when he left for San Francisco Theological Seminary but entrusted me to Susan Abraham's invaluable assistance. I am also grateful to Marian McClure and Will Browne for their support of this project and to my immediate supervisors Maria Arroyo and David Maxwell for generously allowing me to dedicate much time to writing. Jo Ella Holman has also been an important conversation partner. Furthermore, I am grateful for the interest and support of the Association of Presbyterian Mission Pastors and other constituent groups.

The other person who has carefully read and heard me read out loud every word and revision is my Brazilian mission coworker Dirce Naves. Her extremely realistic critique of partnership from the perspective of the southern hemisphere and Latin American culture keeps me painfully honest. She has helped me to view mission work through the eyes of those who have suffered the consequences of our unconscious arrogance and insensitivity. This book would not be authentic without her invaluable assistance. All that she says was reinforced by the students in the Evangelical Theological Community in Chile where I gave an intensive course with the basic contents of the book.

Called as Partners in Christ's Service seeks to help Presbyterians understand and implement their new policy statement and refers to PC(USA) resources and mission work. However, it affirms that God's mission in partnership, by its very nature, must be ecumenical. It is intended for all Christians engaged in mission with God and others. This book, written "from below" in the South, in conversation with mission professors and church leaders in the North, is offered as a theological and practical tool to all in the global church who engage in "re-inventing" partnership in mission for the twenty-first century.

SHERRON KAY GEORGE
Campinas, SP, Brazil
August 12, 2003

PART 1   WHY? Biblical and Theological Foundations of Partnership

"*G*od is love" (1 John 4:8, 16). John tells us that the triune God—Father, Son, and Holy Spirit—is relational. The Trinity is a community of mutuality and reciprocity that reaches out beyond God's self to create and love the world. For this reason, the Church is called to be a community of mutuality and reciprocity that goes beyond itself into the world as a sign of the good news of God's reign of love, peace, and justice.

Partnership is not merely a means, method, or approach to mission. *Partnership is a fundamental dynamic of the triune missionary God of love who is, acts, and relates in mutual partnership in sending the Son, the Spirit, and the church into the world as instruments of God's saving mission.* Just as partnership and mission are part of the essence of the triune God, "'partnership in mission' also belongs to the essence of the Church: partnership is not so much what the Church *does* as what it *is.*" (italics in the original).[1]

"'For God so loved the world that [God] gave his only Son . . .'" (John 3:16). God exists as a loving community of Father, Son, and Holy Spirit, or Creator, Redeemer, and Guide. The Trinity is God's communal expression of love and justice. Love requires self-giving and mutual relationships. God's internal, Trinitarian relationship of love overflows and extends to the world. The world is the stage where God's mission is enacted. The context of discipleship and mission is the world. The mission of God originates in God's heart, God's person, God's activity, God's love. As David Bosch says, "God is a fountain of sending love. This is the deepest source of mission . . . there is mission because God loves people."[2]

The initiative in mission is God's. This can be seen in John 5:19: "'The Son can do nothing on his own, but only what he sees the Father doing; for whatever the Father does, the Son does likewise.'" What is the triune God doing in the world today? God's mission.

Missio Dei (the Latin root for God's mission), is the redemptive activity of the three persons of the Trinity in the world. *Missio Dei* is God's purpose, God's project of life, God's activity, God's intention to establish God's reign in human history and throughout the whole universe. *Missio Dei* is God's movement toward the world. It is for this reason that this book uses "mission" in the singular. God has a mission.

God's mission has a church. Because God is love, God engages in mission in partnerships, in relationships. The first mission partnership, the Trinity, "manifests love by forming a family of equals"[3] and draws them into the partnership. John describes these intimate relationships and mission connections: "'As the Father has loved me, so I have loved you; abide in my love. . . . love one another as I have loved you'" (15:9, 12). Jesus later commissions his disciples to follow him in mission: "'As the Father has sent me, so I send you'" (20:21).

God is a missionary. God has a gracious mission in relation to fallen humanity and all of creation. God's universal saving mission of restoring broken lives and relationships gradually unfolds in human history. God forms a covenant people to be a witness to the nations, sends a Savior to take away the sins of the world, sends the Spirit upon all flesh, and establishes a church that is sent into the world as an instrument of God's mission. The church has not always been a faithful and winsome instrument and has often failed miserably in her task. The "signs" of the reign of God seem veiled by all the violence and suffering around the globe.

Part 1 of this book focuses on the theological foundations of partnership found in God's person and mission, as presented in the Fourth Gospel. The root meaning of the word "mission" is "to send," a key term in John's Gospel. Chapter 1 shows how "God sends the Son into the world." God's mission of restoration, salvation, liberation, and reconciliation is the foundation for the mission of the church. We see in the second chapter that "God sends the church in the power of the Holy Spirit into the world."

Mission, therefore, is not "foreign," is not a program of the church, and is not done by a church committee. The mission frontier is not necessarily geographical. Mission is the responsibility of every baptized Christian in every place. Mission is the identity, reason, and purpose of the church's existence. Mission is done in partnership with God and God's people *in* six continents *by* the church in six continents. *The Church's mission is everything God sends the Church into the world to do, say, and be in response to and participation in God's mission. It includes evangelism, compassionate service, and social justice.*

Chapter 1

Partnership in Mission:
God Sends the Son into the World

"For God so loved the world that [God] gave [God's] only Son, so that everyone who believes in [Jesus] may not perish but may have eternal life. Indeed, God did not send the Son into the world to condemn the world, but in order that the world might be saved through [Jesus]."

—John 3:16–17

The triune missionary God is, relates, and acts in mutual partnership in sending the Son into the world as an instrument of God's saving mission of restoring and transforming broken relationships, lives, and creation.

Trinitarian Partnership in Creation and Redemption

The Word Was with God
John 1:1–18

The writer of the Fourth Gospel tells us in the opening verse, "In the beginning was the Word, and the Word was with God and the Word was God" (1:1). Immediately comes a reaffirmation that the eternal Word was "in the beginning *with* God" (1:2; italics added). "The Greek words *en pros,* which are translated 'was with,' signify a direction and movement: 'was directed toward.' For this reason, some have given the translation 'was face to face with God.'"[1] The Word is defined in relationship with or in the company of God.

From eternity God exists as a community of three equal persons that we call the Trinity. Though distinct, the three persons of the Trinity are always mutually related, and their unity is in their communion. John's Prologue poignantly displays the dynamic eternal relationship of God and the creative Word, whose name is finally disclosed in verse 17: Jesus Christ.

If we compare the beginning of John with the beginning of Genesis, in both we discover that the creation of the world is a work of divine partnership. Furthermore, creation reveals God's self-communicating love and desire for fellowship with the "other."

The self-giving triune missionary God not only speaks and acts to create the world but also redemptively *comes* into the world to enter into a relationship with the people who inhabit it. As Moltmann says, *"The New Testament talks about God by proclaiming in narrative the relationships of the Father, the Son and the Spirit, which are relationships of fellowship and are open to the world"* (italics in the original).[2]

John 1:4 introduces two key themes of the Fourth Gospel: "in him was *life,* and the life was the *light* of all people" (italics added). God is life. God creates life. God gives life. Jesus later says, "'I am the resurrection and the life'" (11:25) and "'I am the way, and the truth, and the life'" (14:6). Jesus declares, "'Just as the living Father sent me, and I live because of the Father, so whoever eats me will live because of me'" (6:57). The purpose of God's creation and of God's saving mission is to give fullness of life to all. Jesus comes "'that they may have life, and have it abundantly'" (10:10). God's mission promotes life and combats every force that denies dignity and fullness of life to any person or group.

In his Prologue John emphasizes the point that "the true light, which enlightens everyone, was coming into the world" (1:9). The light of creation becomes the light of incarnation and finally the light of glory (1:14).[3] The One who is life and light gives life and light to those who follow Jesus, who confirms, "'I am the light of the world. Whoever follows me will never walk in darkness but will have the light of life'" (8:12).

The place of God's mission of love and light is the *world* of human beings. "'For God so loved the world that [God] gave [God's] only Son, so that everyone who believes in [Jesus] may not perish but may have eternal life'" (John 3:16). The triune God of love takes the initiative. God's love gives life. Jesus comes into the world as a gift of God's grace. People can know Jesus, accept him, receive him, and believe in him. The greatest tragedy is that the world which "came into being through" the triune Creator God "did not" and often does not "know" the God of life. Jesus entered history and "came to what was his own, and his own people did not accept him " (1:11). The Creator's love is not forced on the creature, but vulnerably offered. "But to all who received [Jesus], who believed in his name, he gave power to become children of God" (1:12). *Missio Dei* invites a response, an act of reception. Mission invites people to receive God's gracious gifts, to share in God's life and grace: "From [God's] fullness we have all received, grace upon grace" (1:16).

How does the loving Creator approach the creatures? What kind of a relationship does the sovereign divine initiative desire with the world? After all, mission is about God's relationship with God's world, God's movement toward the world, God's openness to the world, God's compassion for the world, God's self-communication of love and hope to the world.

"And the Word became flesh and lived among us" (John 1:14). The eternal divine Word relates to those created by becoming one of us, by taking on and sharing our flesh and bones, by living with us in history, and by identifying with a particular human culture.

God's redemptive mission is incarnational. The Son of God incarnates, enfleshes, embodies human existence. The incarnation is simultaneously an expression of missional partnership between God and God's Son and an invitation to restored relationship between God and God's world. God enters into solidarity with humankind. God's Son participates actively in finite, limited human nature as a poor, fragile, marginal Jewish person. The Word becomes contingency and weakness.

At the same time the Word is none other than "God the only Son, who is close to the Father's heart, who has made [God] known" (1:18). It is obvious that Jesus who is fully God and fully human, eternal and historical, has a close relationship with the Father and with humanity, and that the purpose of his earthly existence is the mission of bringing them together. The earthly Jesus exists as a relationship, a link, a connection, a communication, a mission partnership between God and humanity.

Witness to the Light
John 1:19–34

John the Baptist is introduced in the Prologue as "a man sent from God" (1:6). "He came as a witness to testify to the light" (1:7). The Baptizer becomes the prototype of those who will be "sent" as witnesses to Jesus and God's reign, never pointing to themselves, always in subordination to the One who sends them and of whom they testify. The church is sent into the world as a witness. John humbly points to God's mission in Jesus and identifies himself as only a "voice" (1:23). This brave and humble, self-abasing mission partner is an example for us today. We point not to ourselves or the church's mission, but to God and God's mission.

Jesus' baptism is a symbolic plunge of solidarity with sinful humankind. The humiliation and pain that this act of redemptive solidarity entails is predicted when Jesus is hailed as the sacrificial " 'Lamb of God who takes away the sin of the world' " (John 1:29). His baptism is also an affirmation of the triune mission partnership. The One on whom the Spirit descends and remains " " "is the one who baptizes with the Holy Spirit" ' " (1:33). In the power of the Spirit, Jesus initiates his public ministry.

Jesus Is "Sent" by God

According to the writer of the Fourth Gospel, Jesus thinks of God as a missionary God, a God who sends. John makes forty references to the "sending" of the Son. The Greek words for "sending" are translated into Latin as *missio*, from which we get the word "mission" in English. Jesus understands himself as an instrument "sent" by God into the world to do God's work in partnership with the triune God. Jesus identifies himself as the "one sent by the Father." His missional identity is explicit and compelling. " 'My food is to do the will of him who sent me and to complete his work' " (John 4:34). Jesus emphasizes his equal partnership in God's mission: " 'My Father is still working, and I also am working' " (5:17). His filial relationship is one of mutual knowing and loving, dependence, and willing obedience: " 'The Son can do nothing on his own, but only what he sees the Father doing; for whatever the Father does, the Son does likewise' "(5:19). John's constant references to God as Father are not about gender, but about the intimate family relationship of parent and child.

Jesus' missional prayer at the end of his public ministry, " 'I glorified you on earth by finishing the work that you gave me to do' "(17:4), anticipates his declaration on the cross: " 'It is finished' " (19:30). Jesus accomplished his unique part in *missio Dei,* but God's mission is not yet completed. God is still at work in every nation of the world as initiator and perpetrator of God's mission of salvation, healing, liberation, and reconciliation.

Jesus' self-understanding as one "sent" by God as a participant in God's mission molds the church's self-understanding today as "sent" by God into the world in partnership with the triune God who is still at work in mission. By baptism every Christian has a call, vocation, and commission for mission. All baptized children of God can become coparticipants in God's work. The church today is called to share Jesus' missional identity and determination " 'not to do my own will, but the will of him who sent me' "(6:38). Likewise, we should emulate Jesus' example and speak not on our own, seeking our own glory, but seek only the glory of the One who sends us in mission (7:18). In local and denominational initiatives, we should mirror Jesus' sense of partnership: "'I do nothing on my own, but I speak these things as the Father instructed me. And the one who *sent me* is with me; he has not left me alone, for I always do what is pleasing to him'" (8:28, 29).

The Fourth Gospel leaves no doubt that in mission all initiative, grace, and glory are God's (1:14, 15; 7:18; 8:54; 15:8; 17:4). From Jesus we learn that no one does mission on his or her own. Perhaps the church today should say to the world as Jesus did, "'If I am not doing the works of my Father, then do not believe me. But if I do them, even though you do not believe me, believe the works, so that you may know and understand that the Father is in me and I am in the Father'" (10:37–38). All that the church calls "mission" may not be God's work. It is easy to have mixed motivations and to present one's own personal and cultural projects and advancement as though they were God's. It is tempting to seek one's own gain and glory. Authentic mission points not to the church or to people, but to God and the good news of God's reign.

How, then, does the church discern God's mission, God's plan of life? First, we look attentively around our community, region, and world to see where and how God is at work establishing God's reign of love, justice, and peace. Where is God at work revealing Jesus Christ in a meaningful way to individuals? Where is God at work challenging and eliminating societal structures and attitudes of arrogance and superiority that discriminate, humiliate, and exclude others? Once we discern God's missional activity in a world of emptiness, hopelessness, suffering, and violence, we join in God's mission of evangelism or social justice. This begins in our prayer for others. As we pray, we listen to hear the instructions of the One who sent Jesus and sends us. We then go forth to share the good news, to learn from those whom we encounter, and to share grace in solidarity with others.

Jesus Calls Disciples and Prepares Them to Be "Sent"

Come and See
John 1:35–51

Not only does John portray Jesus as being sent by God but also as calling and preparing disciples and others for participation in God's mission. Jesus' first act of ministry is to call disciples to come and follow him (also his last act in 21:19–22). He invites them to "'Come and see'" (1:39), to companionship in the reign of God, to share an intimate relationship with him, and to "'Follow me'" (1:43). There is no imposition. Only invitation to a lifelong adventure of transformation.

Mission is movement. Following is the first mission movement of disciples who respond to Jesus' gracious invitation. Kirk suggests that "following in the way of Jesus Christ (discipleship) is *the* test of missionary faithfulness."[4] The disciples whom Jesus call in turn invite and bring others. Andrew says to his brother, "'We have found the Messiah'(which is translated Anointed). He brought Simon to Jesus" (1:41–42). Philip invites Nathanael to "'Come and see'" (1:46), and Jesus promises him, "'You will see greater things than these'" (1:50). These evangelistic invitations "gave birth to the community of the disciples of Jesus, men and women destined to bear witness to the God of history."[5]

Following Jesus in mission involves a rhythm of discipleship and apostleship, of continually coming to Jesus and being sent out to bring others to Jesus. Following is not an easy movement for those who are accustomed to the role of leader. Even though the disciples were slow to understand the full implications of following Jesus, they were being prepared to be sent.

Entering One Another's Labor
John 4:1–42

In John 4, during the absence of the disciples, Jesus engages a Samaritan woman in an evangelistic dialogue, she issues an evangelistic invitation to the people in the city, and they are "on their way to [Jesus]" (4:30). The evangelized woman immediately becomes an evangelist in spite of being marginal in several respects. She is from the despised, mixed-Samaritan people who have syncretistic theology and worship. Not only is she a woman, but one of questionable reputation and social status, an unlikely evangelist.

Meanwhile, unaware of God's missional activity, the disciples return with food for Jesus, who replies, "'My food is to do the will of him who sent me and to complete his work'" (4:34). Food sustains life and gives pleasure. Jesus finds nourishment from participating in God's gracious intention for the world, in God's project of life. The phrase "God's work" in the Fourth Gospel refers to God's mission, which makes God's reign a reality in history.

Jesus takes advantage of the teaching moment, employs a common harvest metaphor, and encourages the disciples to "'look around you, and see how the fields are ripe for harvesting'" (4:35). In response to the woman's invitation, were people streaming through the fields? Jesus has already initiated the "eschatological harvest" of abundance, or God's saving mission of calling and gathering in God's people and establishing God's reign of fullness of life, peace, love, and justice for all.

Jesus deepens the missional reflection: "'The reaper is already receiving wages and is *gathering* fruit for eternal life, so that sower and reaper may rejoice *together*'" (4:36; italics added). Who are the sowers and the reapers? It is ambiguous whether sower and reaper are divine or human agents, perhaps because God sends us to join in God's mission work of gathering. However, one thing is certain—God's mission is done in joyful partnerships between "sowers" and "reapers"!

Furthermore, as Mortimer Arias and Alan Johnson put it, "the disciples' mission is derived, dependent, and a gift. . . . It is not original; it is not causative; it is not meritorious work."[6] They go on to say, "The striking message in the missionary paradigm of the harvest is the interrelationship, the fellowship, the unity, and the shared joy of sowers and reapers. Fellowship in mission emerges in these images as a joyful motivation for mission!"[7] Arias and Johnson further comment on "gathering in" and "rejoicing together" and say, "Fellowship and community are the ultimate goal of mission. . . . They are part of a new order of reality, marked by grace, fellowship, and mutual rejoicing. Fellowship is, simultaneously, the means, the end, and the result of mission!" Then they ask, "Can we resonate with the ecumenical dimension of mission, so beautifully anticipated in this missionary imagery of the sowing and reaping and incorporated into the final intercessory prayer of Jesus (4:35–38; 17:20–23)? 'May they be one, so that the world will believe that you sent me'" (17:21 GNB).[8]

To emphasize mission in partnership, Jesus quotes a cultural saying: "'"One sows and another reaps"'" (4:37). Could this proverb be a pessimistic reflection on the inequity of life? If it is, Raymond Brown suggests that "Jesus applies the proverb in an optimistic fashion" to refer to the mission of the disciples.[9] Jesus then says, "'*I sent you* to reap that for which you did not labor. *Others* have labored, and you have *entered into their labor*'" (4:38; italics added). Who are the "others"? Andreas Köstenberger thinks that they "are best taken as Jesus and his predecessors, i.e., the Old Testament prophets up until John the Baptist."[10]

John 4:38 anticipates the commission that will be given in John 17 and 20: "'As the Father has sent me, so I send you'" (17:18 and 20:21). The Savior "sent" by God *sends* the disciples into a collaborative endeavor with God and with other human agents. Disciples follow Jesus to help gather the eschatological harvest. It is awesome and humbling to realize that we *enter into* the mission of the triune God, that we gather for God's future. Partnership is entering into and sharing the work of others and inviting others to enter into and share our work. Mission workers, members of local congregations, and denominational bodies who are constantly entering into the work of others must also be open to having others enter into their work. Otherwise, they are not doing mission in partnership. Mutuality requires openness, hospitality, humility, leadership, and initiative from both parties. If we claim to follow Jesus in mission, we are called to face the problems and risk the dangers of reciprocity and vulnerability.

God's Works Revealed
John 9:1–7

Jesus alludes to the disciples' participation in God's mission again in chapter 9. In reply to an inquiry of the disciples concerning a man born blind, Jesus discloses, "'He was born blind so that God's works might be revealed in him'" (9:3). As in John 4:34, "God's works" or "work" is a metaphor for God's mission or God's project of life. The PC(USA) policy statement "Presbyterians Do Mission in Partnership" defines "mission" in Trinitarian terms as "God's work for the sake of the world God loves. We understand this work to be centered in the Lordship of Jesus Christ and made real through the active and leading power of the Holy Spirit."

John 9:3 subtly suggests that God's sovereign missionary action is greater than and will ultimately triumph over all that has been marred in God's creation. Jesus, however, also affirms human responsibility and participation: "'We must work the works of him who sent me while it is day; night is coming when no one can work. As long as I am in the world, I am the light of the world'" (9:4–5).[11] In a world where so many people are "blind" to the values of God's reign of peace and justice, where the forces of death and violence seem to prevail over life, we *must* seek, recognize, and join "God's works." Jesus nudges the disciples in this direction with another puzzling reference to "greater works" in 14:12.

"Greater Works"
John 14:8–14

In his final missional instructions Jesus says, "'The words that I say to you I do not speak on my own; but the Father who dwells in me *does his works*'" (14:10; italics added). Then he says, "'The one who believes in me will also do the works that I do and, in fact, will do greater works than these, because I am going to the Father'" (14:12). What does "greater" mean? Köstenberger says, "It is Jesus who has done 'the work,' and the disciples will have a part in the greater works the exalted Jesus will perform after his glorification."[12]

Missio Dei is "time-release" mission. It is like a time-release capsule whose medicinal effects continue gradually over time. God's mission continues throughout human history until the final consummation of God's reign over all. God is at work and sends the Son who joins God's mission work, completes his unique part, returns to glory, and sends the disciples to continue God's work in the power of the Spirit. All our "works" are contingent on Jesus' completed redemptive work on earth (cf. 17:4), his ascent "to the Father," and the descent of the Spirit. In his exposition of the Fourth Gospel, *The Light Has Come,* Lesslie Newbigin says,

> The going of Jesus to the Father by the path of suffering, death, and resurrection is the setting in motion of a far vaster movement in which the glory of the Father will be manifested through the works of the disciples done in the name of the Son. The eschatological theme of the mission of the Church to all the nations now begins to open up. The signs of the presence of the reign of God which were given in the ministry of Jesus carried out on the narrow stage of Galilee and Judea will now be multiplied on a far wider stage.[13]

Furthermore, the exalted Lord answers the prayers of disciples-in-mission. Jesus' promises about prayer in John 14:13–14 are connected to the "greater works" he will do through them in mission and not to their personal needs and requests. After all, the final goal of prayer is equipping the Church for mission that results in God's glory. Newbigin puts it in proper perspective: "The glorifying of the Father in the mission of the Church will be the fruit of intercession offered by the Church in the name of Jesus."[14] The vital role of the Spirit in the "greater works" will be seen in the next chapter of this book.

Jesus Teaches Partnership As . . .

John's Gospel can be clearly divided into two parts. In part 1, chapters 1–12, the emphasis is on the mission of Jesus through his "signs" or "works" performed publicly with the purpose of leading the Jews to believe that he is the promised Messiah. These "signs" demonstrate and anticipate God's realm of life and restoration. It reads like a missionary evangelistic tract. The focus in the second part, chapters 13–21, is on the Messiah being "lifted up" (on the cross and in his glorification) and "going" to the Father to enable the continued mission or "greater works" of the exalted Lord through his disciples in the world. Throughout his public ministry Jesus was preparing his disciples to participate in God's mission. However, in chapters 13–17, in a setting of private teaching and intimate fellowship, Jesus intensifies their preparation for this task. His Farewell Discourse (John 14–16) and Missionary Prayer (John 17) look forward to the new mission reality of the disciples and the Church.

Sharing in Love
John 11–13

I see chapters 11–13 as a hinge or bridge between the missions of Jesus and the disciples. In John 11–13 Jesus gives a perfect example of missional praxis (action + reflection). The Lord demonstrates an authentic relationship of giving and receiving, of mutual sharing, suffering, and serving. Jesus shows simply and unequivocally that partnership is LOVE. If mission is following Jesus, then mission is a sharing in the love and grace of God, which enables us to develop a mutual loving partnership with others. Herein is the ideal for which we strive and by which we judge ourselves.

John 11 presents Jesus in the home of his dear friends Martha and Mary, compassionately sharing their grief because of the death of Lazarus. Martha confesses, " 'I believe that you are the Messiah, the Son of God, the one *coming into the world*' "(11:27; italics added). Jesus was so disturbed that he wept (11:35), for he loved Lazarus deeply (11:36). After personally participating in their pain, Jesus ministered the gift of restored life. The resurrection of Lazarus is the climactic sign in John 1–12. It reminds us that the purpose of Jesus' mission is to give fullness of life to all—satisfying, abundant, eternal life that begins here and now.

In the next chapter Jesus again receives hospitality and partakes of table fellowship, at which time Mary[15] expresses gratitude for Jesus' gift of life to her brother. By anointing Jesus' feet with costly perfume and drying them with her hair, she responds to his gift by giving of herself and also anticipates and shares the pain of his passion. Jesus receives her anointing, her ministry, her gift to him. It is a relationship of mutuality.

Jesus enters Jerusalem, conscious of the fact that the seemingly enthusiastic welcome is no indication of what "this hour" holds for him. To the Greeks he indicates that by his death and glorification (by being "lifted up"), he will bear "much fruit" (12:24, 32). He adds, " 'Whoever serves me must follow me' " (12:26) and, like Mary, die to self-interest and practice self-sacrifice and loving service. Following Jesus in mission is costly and risky.

Once more at table in chapter 13 Jesus imitates Mary's humble loving service and washes the disciples' feet. Peter has difficulty receiving and accepting the radical reversal of roles, so Jesus explains, " 'Unless I wash you, you have no share with me' " (13:8). The Greek expression *echein meros* can mean "to share with; be a partner with" or, even more, to have a "share" or "heritage" with.[16] Partnership is *sharing in love*. Partnership is *sharing in grace*. We not only have fellowship with Jesus, but our God-given "heritage" is to share God's eternal life, love, and mission. *We are heirs to God's grace in Jesus Christ.*

Mary and Jesus show that incarnational mission entails embodiment. We wash. We eat. We weep, laugh, dance, and sing. We touch. Our God, who is love, embraces, feels, communicates, and heals. Mission is self-emptying, self-giving, and other-receiving. Embodied love begins with mutual recognition, mutual respect, mutual sharing, and mutual serving, and it extends to mutual suffering.

After reversing the world's normal pattern of authority and demonstrating humble mission service, Jesus articulates "'a new commandment, that you love one another. Just as I have loved you, you also should love one another. By this everyone will know that you are my disciples, if you have love for one another'" (John 13:34; 15:12, 17). John's Gospel comes full circle. Those who receive God's love then give God's love and continue to receive it from others. We enter into the flowing movement of God's compassion for the world.

Bearing Fruit
John 15:1–17

In chapter 15, as in John 4:35–38, Jesus employs an agricultural metaphor to describe the disciples' participation in God's mission: "'I am the vine, you are the branches. Those who abide in me and I in them bear much fruit, because apart from me you can do nothing'" (15:5). Chapter 12 refers to the fruit Jesus bears (v. 24); chapter 14 looks forward to "greater works" (v. 12) through the disciples; in chapter 15 the disciples are united into the relationship of love between Father and Son; and in 15:16 Jesus explicitly commissions the disciples "to go and bear fruit, fruit that will last." "Fruit," then, is immediately linked to prayer and the command to love one another. Mission, therefore, is the result of a dependent partner relationship with the triune God, a relationship of friends (15:13–15). Authentic partnership leads to friendship. We cannot do mission alone. There simply is no fruitful mission without mutual partnership, mutual indwelling, mutual abiding. Partnership is "abiding" in God, living in the presence and grace of God, prayerfully participating in God's mission, seeking first God's will and kingdom values. God's love is the source, foundation, motivation, and direction of mission. God's love and judgment refine and purify our missionary actions.

Following Jesus
John 21:15–23

In the first chapter of the Fourth Gospel Jesus calls people to follow him (1:35–43). In chapter 10 he states that he is the "good shepherd" and that "his sheep" follow him. Discipleship in 12:24–26 means following even at great cost. In chapter 13 Jesus gives an example to be emulated, foretells his betrayal, refers to his "going" away, and then exhorts his followers to " 'love one another. Just as I have loved you, you also should love one another' " (13:34, 35). Peter responds, " 'Lord, where are you going?' " Jesus answers, " 'Where I am going, you cannot follow me now; but you will follow afterward' " (13:36). Peter replies, " 'Lord, why can I not follow you now? I will lay down my life for you' " (13:37). Jesus answers that, rather than following, Peter will deny him three times. The prerequisites to all mission activities are following Jesus and loving others. This is no easier for us than it was for Peter, and the Church has failed repeatedly.

However, John ends the Gospel with hope and assurance that God's mission will be continued by faltering and vulnerable instruments. After denying his Lord three times, Peter thrice affirmatively answers Jesus' question, " 'Do you love me?' " Jesus in turn commands, " 'Feed my lambs. . . . Tend my sheep. . . . Feed my sheep' " (21:15–17). Sheep (followers) become shepherds, but they never cease to be sheep. For this reason, Jesus' final words to the missionary community recipient of the Fourth Gospel are " 'Follow me!' " (21:19, 22). We follow and share in the love and mission of God until Christ's return. Love indeed is the driving force of every genuine mission partnership.

Chapter 2

Partnership in Mission:
God Sends the Church into the World
in the Power of the Holy Spirit

The Church is called to be Christ's faithful evangelist going into the world, making disciples of all nations.

—Book of Order

"As the Father has sent me, so I send you."

—John 20:21

The triune missionary God is, relates, and acts in mutual partnership in send-ing the Church in the power of the Spirit into the world as an instrument of God's saving mission of restoring broken relationships, lives, and creation. As God sent Jesus and the Spirit, so God sends the Church into the world as one agent of God's missionary purpose (John 17:18; 20:21). Jürgen Molt-mann explains, "Through the sending of the creative Spirit, the trinitarian his-tory of God becomes a history that is open to the world, open to men and women, and open to the future. Through the experience of the life-giving Spirit in faith, in baptism, and in the fellowship of believers, people are inte-grated into the history of the Trinity."[1] This means that by the Spirit who "indwells" all Christians, we are integrated into God's mission.

Jesus promised his disciples that the Spirit "will testify on my behalf" and further charged them, "You also are to testify because you have been with me from the beginning" (John 15:26, 27). After Jesus "goes away," God sends the Spirit whom Jesus calls the Helper, the Spirit of truth, the Com-forter, the Companion (John 14:26; 15:26; 16:13; 20:22). When the Spirit "descends" upon the 120 women and men gathered on the day of Pentecost (see Acts 2), the church is born to be a "witness" (Acts 1:8). The church would not exist nor engage in God's work in the world apart from the Holy Spirit's presence and empowerment. Karl Barth develops his ecclesiology (doctrine of the church) around the missionary nature of the church, which "exists in being sent and in building up itself for the sake of its mission."[2] Barth portrays the Holy Spirit gathering in, building up, and sending out the Christian community.[3]

The Fourth Gospel was written near the end of the first century to provide instructions to a faith community that exists as a result and continuation of the mission partnership of the triune God and the early disciples. They probably have been excluded from the synagogue because of their zealous missionary activity, but are still trying to convince Jews and Gentiles of Jesus' identity as God, the Savior of the world. A careful reading of John's Gospel gives us a glimpse of the early church's self-understanding that can guide the church-in-mission today.

The Early Church Understands Itself As . . .

A Worshiping Community That Gathers for Word and Sacrament

The Fourth Gospel is addressed to a worshiping community. This is evident in the dialogue of Jesus with the Samaritan woman in John 4. Beginning with Jesus' need and request " 'Give me a drink' " (4:7), they proceed through a gift exchange involving thirst and water. In the process they transcend cultural hostilities and establish a mutual relationship.

The conversation turns to ethnic and worship controversies. Where is the proper place to worship? Jesus deals respectfully with the historical ethnic realities and moves beyond the issue of sacred space and place to the centrality of worship. He says, " 'But the hour is coming, and is now here, when the true worshipers will worship the Father in spirit and truth, for the Father seeks such as these to worship him. God is spirit, and those who worship [God] must worship in spirit and truth' " (4:23, 24). Obviously, God desires, seeks, forms, and is pleased with a worshiping community of reconciled differences.

The Samaritan woman's witness, coupled with Martha's confession, " 'Yes, Lord, I believe that you are the Messiah, the Son of God, the one coming into the world' " (11:27), remind us that the worshiping community is a confessional church. The Gospel of John was "written so that you may come to believe that Jesus is the Messiah, the Son of God, and that through believing you may have life in his name" (20:31). This is why every Sunday in services of worship around the world Protestants and Catholics use the words of the ancient Nicene Creed or Apostles' Creed to publicly confess what they believe about the triune God.

John's account of Jesus' baptism (1:32, 33) and Jesus' insistence with Nicodemus that " 'no one can enter the kingdom of God without being born of water and Spirit'" (3:5) suggest that the worshiping church that confesses faith in Jesus Christ is a sacramental community defined, constituted, commissioned, and united by the ecclesial practice of baptism. Furthermore, the baptismal community that gathers to be nurtured and built up by Word (8:47; 15:3, 7; 17:8) and sacrament is thereby transformed, equipped, and empowered for mission. Facets of this baptismal rebirth and transformation for mission in partnership can be seen in these words:

> The practice of baptism introduces persons into a radically new kind of social relationship; no longer isolated individuals, they have become brothers and sisters adopted into the body of Christ to live a communal life as a sign of God's reign in the midst of human history. Incorporation into Christ involves movement from the alienating independence of competitive and self-interested individualism to the affirming interdependence of a community grounded in the obedience and self-giving of Jesus Christ. . . . Consequently, democratic principles and values are not the basis for Christian equality—baptism is the basis.[4]

In John 6 it is apparent that the baptismal community that the Fourth Gospel addresses is also a eucharistic community that takes bread, gives thanks, and distributes it sacramentally and missionally. The community receives limited resources (a child's contribution), experiences a transformation of those resources, shares them with others, and sees that no resources are wasted (gathers the leftovers). As Anthony Gittens says, "The eucharist is all about transformations . . . the transformation of the worshiping community, of the worshiper, and of society as a whole."[5] We do not transform anyone. Only God, who is mysteriously at work by the Spirit, transforms. God's grace operates through Word and sacraments. As we go forth in mission, it is essential to remember that "society must be transformed from *within*. We have to discover the values of others, and as missioners in honest and respectful dialogue, call them (and be called!) in the name of Jesus to a new response: a transformation."[6]

However, transformation through mission and sacrament is a process. We spend all of our lives discovering the significance and experiencing the transformative impact of our baptism and eucharistic participation. The crowd who received the bread from Jesus did not fully understand. Jesus explains God's missional project of life: "'The bread of God is that which comes down from heaven and gives life to the world'" (6:33). Jesus then explicitly asserts, "'I am the bread of life'" (6:35, 48). The God of life is present with the community in the Eucharist or Lord's Supper. Furthermore, through the sacraments the worshiping community not only receives life but is drawn into the triune mission partnership that gives life: " 'Those who eat my flesh and drink my blood *abide in me*, and *I in them*. Just as the living Father sent me, and I live because of the Father, so whoever eats me will live because of me' " (6:56, 57; italics added). These verses echo the theme of the covenant by affirming "the mutual indwelling of God (and Jesus) and the Christian" in the Lord's Supper, and they further make the amazing claim that when we "eat and drink" we receive *"a share in God's own life"* (italics in the original).[7] Because we share God's life and grace, later Jesus repeats the same phrase, " 'as the Father has sent me,' " and adds, " 'so I send you' " (20:21).

In the Presbyterian Church (U.S.A.)'s Directory for Worship, we find the clear connection between Word, sacrament, and mission: "The worshiping community in its integrity before the Word and its unity in prayer and Sacraments is a sign of the presence of the reign of God. . . . God calls the church in worship to join the mission of Jesus Christ in service to the world. As it participates in that mission the church is called to worship God in Jesus Christ, who reigns over the world."[8]

A Missional Community That Is Sent into the World

The recipient community of John's Gospel understands itself as a body of people "sent" in the power of the Spirit to continue God's mission in the world.

The first part of the Fourth Gospel, chapters 1–12, focuses on Jesus' mission through his "signs" and "works." The second part, chapters 13–21, concerns the preparation of the disciples to continue the mission of Jesus after his death and resurrection.

What are the elements Jesus includes in the disciples' missionary orientation? We have seen that it does not begin in the classroom, but with Jesus' example of humble service in the foot washing (chapter 13). This is followed by his Farewell Discourse to his disciples, which contains vital instructions for those who will engage in mission in the power of the Spirit (chapters 14–16). The culminating point is Jesus' Missionary Prayer (chapter 17).

In his Farewell Discourse Jesus foresees the completion of his mission (through his death and resurrection) and the transfer of God's "time-release" mission to the church. He declares, " 'Now I am going to him who sent me' " (16:5) and promises the disciples that the Father and Son will send the Helper, the Spirit of truth, to be with them and in them to teach, equip, enable, transform, and guide them in God's mission (14:26; 15:26, 27; 16:13). In the power of the Holy Spirit, the third person of the holy Trinity, God's mission goes on through the church. The Christian community is utterly dependent on the Spirit in mission.

After assuring the disciples that the Spirit will be sent, Jesus assumes the role of intercessor in mission. In Jesus' great Missionary Prayer in John 17, he first identifies himself as the missionary sent by God (vv. 1–5), as a partner in God's mission who will now "glorify" the Father on earth "by finishing" his unique part (17:4). God's mission, however, has not been completed.

In the second part of his prayer, Jesus intercedes for the disciples who will be sent in mission (vv. 6–19). It is interesting to note the importance of the Word of God that is graciously given to the disciples. They receive and believe God's Word, which comes to them through the Trinitarian mission partnership. The Word consecrates and sanctifies them. The Word initiates mission and transforms lives. Only a worshiping community that is nourished by Word and sacrament is sent out in mission.

Jesus makes it clear that the disciples participate in his sanctification by the Word and in his mission partnership with God in the world. This means they share both his joy and the pain of his rejection. In his prayer Jesus anticipates the commissioning of the church: "'As you have sent me into the world, so I have sent them into the world'" (17:18). The church, therefore, is a community *sent* on a mission to, for, and with the world.

John 20 narrates the appearance of the risen Lord on the evening of the resurrection to the disoriented fearful disciples behind closed doors, the antithesis of mission. Jesus greets them with a solemn commission: "'Peace be with you. As the Father has sent me, so I send you'" (20:21). He then breathes on them as a sign of their empowerment and a seal of their inclusion in the triune mission partnership and says, "'Receive the Holy Spirit'" (20:22). By the power of the Spirit, those timid disciples were transformed into the worshiping missional community to whom the Fourth Gospel was written.

A closer analysis of the "great commission" in John 20:19–23 reminds us that the marks of the sent-church include peace, suffering, and forgiveness. The risen Lord who brought peace to the troubled disciples also "showed them his hands and his side" (20:20). We can never forget the risk and the cost involved in God's mission. Surely God still suffers and weeps upon contemplating the violence, arrogance, suffering, and injustice in our world. In the power of the Spirit, the Lamb of God who takes away the sin of the world exhorted his followers, "'If you forgive the sins of any, they are forgiven them'" (20:23). We must demonstrate the good news of God's forgiveness in our relationships with all people and also pray constantly, "Forgive us our sins, as we forgive those who sin against us."

If the church today is sent into the world as Jesus was, we too must be in solidarity with the pain of the excluded in our cities and around the world. We, as followers of the crucified One, have no guarantee of security, success, comfort, and popularity. We must be ready to humble ourselves as individuals, races, churches, and nations and ask forgiveness for our sins. In our encounters with "others" who are different, we must communicate forgiveness. Are we ready today to search ourselves and see if these signs are truly present in our mission work?

Today's Church Is a Witness to Christ and a Sign of God's Reign *When* It . . .

"The Church is called to be a sign in and for the world of the new reality which God has made available to people in Jesus Christ."[9] We call this new reality the kingdom, realm, or reign of God. It is a reign of love, justice, and peace. Every act and word of the incarnate Lord was a sign of the inbreaking of God's new reality on earth.

Practices Relationships of Mutual Love

When the church follows Christ in mission and embodies the same incarnational love of God, the church is a sign and sacrament of God's mission and reign. The central theme of this book is our commitment to participate in God's mission through partnerships and to the practice of partnership in mission. The ground and fountain of *missio Dei* is the triune God of love. God's mission, which emanates from love and flows forth into the world in love, consistently is accomplished in partnerships. Therefore, mission partnerships within the denomination and with other churches, Christian communities, institutions, and organizations inside and outside the United States must be born, continually refined, and ruled by love.

What does practicing relationships of mutual love entail? Our ideal and goal must be partnerships of equality, mutuality, reciprocity, and solidarity. However, the realities in today's world cause doubts and cynicism in relation to our ideals. Is it possible for poor and rich churches or for small and large denominations to be equal partners with equal status? Do asymmetrical relationships of power annihilate authentic partnerships? It is easy for the poor to be in solidarity with the poor and to give sacrificially. Is it possible for the rich and powerful to be in solidarity with the poor and powerless? Maybe, but it is very difficult and perhaps constitutes the greatest challenge before us in mission today. Attitudes of cultural, national, or religious superiority and isolationism make mutuality and solidarity impossible.

Do we know how to love and be loved by partner churches? Love begins with the recognition and acceptance of others as human beings with dignity, as subjects of God's love. Those who do not love and respect others do not love themselves or God. Love cultivates mutual sharing, mutual serving, and mutual forgiveness, and extends to mutual suffering. Love is not feeling sorry for, offering charity to, or taking advantage of the vulnerability or generosity of others. It means weeping with those who weep, feeling the humiliation of the humiliated, and coming alongside those who with dignity struggle for basic needs and rights. Somehow we must try to feel what others feel and to experience what others experience, and these are arduous tasks in our selfish, individualistic culture. Too often we perform mission tasks only with our hands and not with our hearts. We don't take the time to "walk in the others' shoes," to listen respectfully to and understand the others' perspective. Our tendency is to "fix" problems rather than to experience their impact and seek their root causes, of which we might be a part.

Mission in Christ's way is discovering the mystery of the incarnation, "the Word became flesh and lived among us" (1:14). In chapter 1 we contemplated Jesus' embodiment of mutual love as recorded in the incidents in John 11–13. He wept with his grieving friends. At table in their home in Bethany and with his disciples in Jerusalem, Jesus received and gave symbols of loving service. The culminating missional instructions that Jesus gave to the disciples on the night that he was betrayed serve as a directive for all partnerships: " 'I give you a new commandment, that you love one another. Just as I have loved you, you also should love one another. By this everyone will know that you are my disciples, if you have love for one another' " (John 13:34, 35).

If people can let down their defenses and relax informally around a common table with a common vision and goals, they have the opportunity to transcend past mistakes in mission and practice partnerships of love. Members of particular congregations who gather around tables of fellowship with partners who are very different from them can experience the miracle of being equals in giving and receiving gifts of love, peace, forgiveness, and joy.

Seeks and Practices Unity

When we practice mutual love, it is natural that we seek to practice unity. Love unites. Mission unites. After all, the gospel is universal—for all and bonding all. The theme of the universality of God's mission can be traced throughout John's Gospel, beginning in the Prologue. The Word who is life and brings life comes into the world as "the light of all people" (1:4). John testifies "so that all might believe through him" (1:7). God so loved the world (3:16), and the Messiah is the "Savior of the world" (4:42).

The Fourth Gospel uses two corporate metaphors to refer to the church or shared life in a worshiping missional community that is a witness by presence, works, and words in the world. The metaphors are "flock" (chapter 10 and 21:15) and "branches" (chapter 15), both of which imply unity.

In chapter 10 of John, Jesus declares, "'I am the good shepherd'" (10:11, 14). He is the Shepherd-Teacher who calls, gathers, leads, teaches, and models. Jesus makes clear the purpose of his mission to the sheep: "'I came that they may have life, and have it abundantly'" (10:10). God offers fullness of life to all. In order to do this, Jesus gave his life for the sheep (10:11, 15, 17, 18; 15:13). Sheep listen to and follow Jesus in discipleship and mission. He states, "'My sheep hear my voice. I know them, and they follow me'" (10:27). This involves coming in, going out, finding pasture, and bringing in other sheep (10:9, 16). Sheep live together in flocks. They are not individualistic loners.

The ecumenical overtones gain force when Jesus further enunciates, "'I have other sheep that do not belong to this fold. I must bring them also, and they will listen to my voice. So there will be one flock, one shepherd'" (10:16). While we cannot define with precision the nature and identity of the "other sheep," we must be open, respectful, and expectant to God's presence in our neighbor who is different in theology, ethnicity, sexual orientation, or faith commitment.

After emphasizing the intimate relation between the sheep and the shepherd and between the sheep who will be gathered in "one flock," John returns to a favorite theme of the Fourth Gospel: the partnership of the Father and Son in *missio Dei*. When in John 10:30 Jesus states, "'The Father and I are one [together],'" he is talking about their "operational" unity in the mission of giving life. Brazilian theologian Leonardo Boff points out that the Greek word translated "one" (*hen*) is not the numerical number (*heis*). It literally means "together" and appears again in 10:38: "'the Father is [together] in me and I am [together] in the Father.'" Their union "does not erase difference and individuality . . . the union presupposes difference. By love and reciprocal communion they are one, the only God-love."[10] Their unity is for the sake of God's mission of gathering humankind into God's fullness of life.

It is crystal clear in the Fourth Gospel that just as the persons of the Trinity are one together in mission, so the church both in its worship and in its mission is to be "one flock," an ecumenical community. The PC(USA) *Book of Order* states, "The unity of the Church is a gift of its Lord and finds expression in its faithfulness to the mission to which Christ calls it. . . . Visible oneness, by which a diversity of persons, gifts, and understandings is brought together, is an important sign of the unity of God's people. . . . The Presbyterian Church (U.S.A.) . . . is willing to seek and to maintain communion and community with all other branches of the one, catholic Church."[11]

If the metaphor of the "flock" demonstrates the corporate and universal dimensions of the worshiping missional community, the metaphor of the "vine" and the "branches" in John 15 reinforces it. The partnership of Jesus, the "vine," and the Father, the "vinedresser" is evident. The unity between Jesus and his disciples, the "branches," is striking. We are nurtured, corrected, and strengthened by "abiding" and become participants in Jesus and in God's mission of "bearing fruit." Clearly, branches are not only dependent on the vine but intricately related to one another. There are no solitary living branches.

It is imperative that we recognize our failures and limitations and our need for other "branches" of the Christian church. The PC(USA) policy statement articulates, "Recognizing our human limitations and because of our fundamental unity in Jesus Christ, we believe we are called to mission in the discipline of partnership." Furthermore, the statement says, "Partnership is based on the fundamental belief that God's love for the world is greater than any one church can possibly comprehend or realize." Because of this, "We may join around a common goal with other churches, with secular organizations, or with other faith communities," seeking, receiving, and practicing the gift of unity.

The culmination of the ecumenical commitment to the practice of unity comes in the last part of Jesus' Missionary Prayer in John 17 when he turns to "those who will believe" (17:20). Is Jesus envisioning an expansion of God's mission partnership to include those who do not yet believe? Listen reflectively to his prayer:

> "I ask not only on behalf of these [who are being sent as missionaries], but also on behalf of those who will believe in me through their word [verbal evangelism with a message], that they may all be one. As you, Father, are in me and I am in you, may they also be in us [mystical unity in God's universal mission], so that the world may believe that you have sent me. . . . I in them and you in me, that they may become completely one, so that the world may know that you have sent me and have loved them even as you have loved me." —John 17:20–23

These verses point to the missionary purpose or goal of Trinitarian and Christian unity and fellowship. The communion and unity of the Trinity is an "open" unity, always open to others. It is an invitational unity, always inviting all creatures and all of creation to embrace God's project of life. Through the unity, word, witness, action, and lifestyle of the church today, is the world coming to believe that God sent Jesus to redeem, restore, and liberate all of creation? Or are our selfish imperialistic actions, our aggressive unilateralism that has undermined the United Nations, and our disunity in the church causing the world to question the legitimacy of our Christian institutions and faith?

Mission and discipleship are not individual but corporate endeavors. Unity and partnership in a faith community of disciples are indispensable for mission. Mutual love and unity within the church universal are foundational for mission to the world. The relationship of unity and love between Father and Son is the model and source of our unity. We are brought into the Trinitarian unity and love.

The church that was born in Jerusalem on the day of Pentecost is now a truly global church doing mission on six continents. We join Christians who recite the Nicene Creed in hundreds of languages and affirm that all local congregations together form the "one holy catholic apostolic church." The church is both "catholic" (because there is one universal global church) and "particular" (because there are many local congregations).[12]

The PC(USA)'s partner relationships with ecumenical councils and agencies, General Assembly agencies, partner denominations, institutions, and presbyteries remind us that each local congregation shares in and needs the full catholicity of the universal church. Robert J. Schreiter teaches us that catholicity in today's globalized world means that each local community is a part of the global church and only finds wholeness and fullness of faith through intercultural exchange and communication with other communities.[13] Leonardo Boff insists that the catholicity of the church points to our responsibility to respect and receive the spiritual gifts and particularities of other congregations.[14]

In communion with the saints of the worshiping missional church to whom the Fourth Gospel was written at the end of the first century and with our partners-in-mission around the globe and the denomination, may we seek earnestly to practice incarnational love and to demonstrate the "oneness" of the whole church for the glory of God who is a community of three in one.

PART 2   HOW? Attitudes of Partnership

---

*P*art 1 affirms that *partnership is a fundamental dynamic of the triune mis-sionary God of love who is, acts, and relates in mutual partnership in sending the Son, the Spirit, and the church into the world as instruments of God's sav-ing mission.* We talked about God's love as the source of *missio Dei,* which finds expression in mission partnerships of love. We observed in the Gospel of John the manner in which Jesus displayed a loving partnership with the Father. The Johannine Jesus says, " 'The Father is in me and I am in the Father' " (John 10:38). In like manner, John defines Jesus by his relationships with others. Jesus demonstrated relationships of mutual love with his friends Mary, Martha, and Lazarus and with his disciples, one of whom is identified as the Beloved Disciple, "the one whom Jesus loved" (John 13:23; 20:2; 21:7). The intimate relationship between the "vine" and the "branches" enables disciples to love one another and bear fruit that glorifies God (John 15:1–17).

The mission of the triune God of love is holistic and universal. God sends the *whole* church into the *whole* world with the *whole* gospel, which has implications for the *whole* person and the *whole* inhabited earth. God's good news affects the physical, mental, emotional, spiritual, cultural, and social life both of those who proclaim it and of those who hear it. God's mission of good news is personal, relational, and structural. The global church engages in God's holistic mission through evangelism, compassionate service, social justice, common mission, ecumenism, and interfaith dialogue. Presbyterians excel in actions of service and often struggle for appropriate ways to practice evangelism and justice in today's world. Historically, we have been leaders in the ecumenical movement and in interfaith dialogue and witness. What are some of our cutting edge challenges in mission today?

As we seek to be faithful followers of Jesus, we initially tend to think of mission in terms of "doing good," "helping others," or "giving donations."

How do we move beyond these starters to a more holistic understanding of God's mission in today's changing world?

In order to help the early Christian community understand God's mission, the Fourth Gospel sets the stage with the calling of Jesus' first followers in John 1. Chapter 2 narrates Jesus' first "sign," turning water into wine, which was indeed an act of "doing good" and "helping others." This sign also "revealed [God's] glory," the goal of all mission, and through it, Jesus' "disciples believed in him" (John 2:11). However, Jesus' next public act was to critique the religious leaders and cleanse the temple, which had been commercialized (John 2:13–22). Throughout his ministry, Jesus continued to critique and correct both his disciples and the religious establishment.

When the curtain opens for the second part of the Fourth Gospel, Jesus is humbly and respectfully washing the feet of his disciples. After he finished, Jesus says, "'I have set you an example, that you also should do as I have done to you'" (John 13:15). Jesus furthermore exhorts them, "'I give you a new commandment, that you love one another. Just as I have loved you, you also should love one another. By this everyone will know that you are my disciples, if you have love for one another'" (John 13:34, 35). As Christ's disciples, our goal and ideal is to practice mission in partnership following the "example" and "attitudes" of Christ, to practice mission "just as" we see our compassionate Lord modeling it. We are painfully aware that our dreams and ideals are distant from what we do. For this reason we are dependent on God's Spirit, who continually calls, encourages, corrects, forgives, and redirects us.

God progressively moves us to a deeper comprehension of God's project of fullness of life. Often the church has the best of intentions and undertakes legitimate mission activity, but proceeds in ways that confuse the gospel message and do not dignify people and glorify God. Usually this is quite unintentional and because of one's culture.

The church is a sign and sacrament of God's reign when it practices mutual affection and unity. The church is called to participate in mission in Christ's way through partner relationships of mutual love. How do we allow God's infinite love to be the motivating and guiding force in our mission partnerships? Where does the process of growth, renewal, and obedience in mission begin? The relationships that are part of God's person and mission require the cultivation of certain attitudes. As they participated in "God's works" together, Jesus and his disciples demonstrated the attitudes entailed in doing mission in partnership. In order to emulate the incarnational model of God's Trinitarian mission, all partnerships today must intentionally include an honest and critical reflection on missional attitudes. More important than what we do, give, or say is *how* we do it.

The thesis of Part 2 is: *"Being" or attitudes must undergird all partner relationships and missional practices together.* I invite you to open yourself to the renewing winds of the Spirit and to consider from a fresh perspective three foundational missional attitudes in the next three chapters: respect, compassion, and humility. In chapter 3 we will focus on respect, our attitude toward others. What does it mean to respect the *whole* person, other cultures, and God's creation? Chapter 4 explores compassion—an emotional, affective missional attitude that flows from one's inner being and guides our response to the needs of others. We turn in chapter 5 to humility, our attitude toward ourselves. May our Shepherd-Teacher guide, convert, equip, and transform us as we examine our attitudes and motives in mission.

Chapter 3

Missional Attitudes: Respect

Partnership calls all partners to respect other partners in Christ, and to recognize one another's equal standing before God.
                                                        —PC(USA) policy statement

The Samaritan woman said to [Jesus], "How is it that you, a Jew, ask a drink of me, a woman of Samaria?"
                                                        —John 4:9

The open and respectful manner in which Jesus approached and treated the woman at the well in Samaria was a shock to her, her Samaritan townsfolk, Jesus' Jewish disciples, and the readers of the Fourth Gospel. Cultural attitudes of mutual hostility and separation were superceded by attitudes of acceptance and reconciliation. The "living water" that Jesus offered to her confirmed and dignified her being. Later Jesus promised that the streams of "living water" that flow forth in mission from the triune God will give life and dignity to all (John 7:37–39). In chapter 3 of John's Gospel, Jesus' dialogue with Nicodemos, the Jewish religious leader who "came to Jesus by night," was equally respectful. In Jesus we find a model of love and respect.

Created in God's Image

Respect for the dignity of every human being as a person created in God's image—regardless of race, ethnicity, gender, economic status, ideology, and religion—is fundamental in all mission and in all of life. In Genesis 1 we learn that "God created humankind in [God's] image, in the image of God he created them; male and female [God] created them" (1:27). God blesses the man and woman and entrusts them with coresponsibility over all of creation. The stewards of the earth are honored, respected, and enjoyed by the Creator who walks and talks with them.

God's gracious saving mission begins in Genesis 3 with the call "Where are you?" (3:9). When they heard God's voice, Adam and Eve, filled with shame because of their disobedience, hid themselves. In like manner, we are ashamed of the ways we have marred God's image in us. Our failure to respect and reflect the divine image in ourselves and in our sister and brother is ever before us. In our daily struggle with the temptations that spring from our sinful nature, we are in constant need of God's grace and forgiveness. Our hope is rekindled when we see in Genesis 3 the promises of our just and loving God. A very significant detail in the saga is that the Maker continues to treat the rebellious creatures with dignity by clothing them with garments of skins.

Psalm 139 portrays God forming and knitting the human being together in the mother's womb. The psalmist marvels, "I praise you, for I am fearfully and wonderfully made. Wonderful are your works" (139:14). In more colloquial terms, God makes no junk; God makes no trash. Every human being on the planet is equally created in God's image and likeness. There is no superior race, culture, religion, or nation in God's creation. In Christ there is no rich or poor, no black or white, no north or south, no east or west. This does not mean that we lose or despise our distinctive identities as persons and nations, but that all people are given the same intrinsic value by our Creator. Since God creates all humans in God's image, we are called to treat each other with respect. After all, if we do not respect others, can we really respect the divine Other who created them? Respect is a basic human right that is not earned or based on merit. God's image in all is a gift.

Subjects, Not Objects

In accord with the Biblical teaching on the image of God, a basic tenet of the Brazilian educator Paulo Freire's pedagogy is that all God's human creatures are *subjects,* and no one should be treated as an *object.* The oppressed are subjects of their own liberation. Students are subjects of their own learning. Nations are subjects of their own building. God creates people to act responsibly, not to be acted upon. As God's human creatures we are all "subjects" in our shared history, community, and world. We are agents who make, mold, and write human history.

However, we can never forget that creatures are "junior subjects" created by a loving Creator who is the eternal Subject. Presbyterians believe both in the sovereign rule of God over time and history and in the active participation of humankind in history. We believe that God is a community-of-three and a covenant-making God who calls a covenant community to become "subjects" and "partners" with the triune God. Nonetheless, it is important to remember, as Shirley Guthrie reminds us, that we are "unlikely partners" in God's mission, *"no more qualified for the job than anyone else"* (italics in the original).[1] Furthermore, we are "junior partners" and "servant partners." Guthrie explains, *"To be God's chosen partners is to be God's servants in the world, not God's privileged elite or God's storm troopers"* (italics in the original).[2] We know that in God's unsearchable wisdom and freedom, God also works through people outside the covenant community who have equal dignity and deserve equal respect.

The implications of this are immense. Because all human beings created in God's image are active subjects and not passive objects, no person should be abused, used, exploited, manipulated, or controlled by another person under any circumstance. Violence occurs whenever people are treated as objects to be dominated. Examples abound, from sexual abuse to terrorist attacks to atrocities of war.

The ways persons are treated as objects are more subtle in mission. When individuals, churches, or nations are helped, lifted up, or pitied, they are being treated as objects. No mutual gift exchange occurs. Paternalism is a form of benevolent violence and lack of respect. People maintain their dignity when they are enabled and empowered with opportunities to help and develop themselves. Even in evangelism, people should never be manipulated or coerced as objects. We share the liberating news of the gospel respectfully and invite people to respond freely. People should not be seen as objects of evangelism or development to be converted, "fixed," or changed. No person converts or changes anyone. Only God converts, heals, and transforms those who accept the offer of grace and enables them "both to will and to work for [God's] good pleasure" (Phil. 2:13).

Human beings created in God's image are subjects/agents in history with self-identity and the basic human characteristics of dignity and autonomy. When a person suffers the loss of food, home, employment, family, or friends, sometimes only personal dignity remains. Latin Americans have taught me that dignity is the most important gift a person possesses. In living and in dying, God's creatures are entitled to dignity. Perhaps there is no greater sin than disrespect for the dignity of others.

Autonomy with Limits

The opening chapters of Genesis show us that those created in God's image receive a certain degree of autonomy. God respects our freedom to make choices and allows us to live with the consequences. However, there are limits to one's autonomy. The first and foremost limit to our free will is God's absolute freedom. As finite creatures we are utterly dependent on our infinite Creator. We believe that God is love and that we were created for a loving and obedient relationship with the divine Other. Where there is love and respect, absolute autonomy does not exist. God freely limited God's own freedom by creating creatures who were *different* from the triune God and by entering into a caring relationship of copartners and cocreators with them.

Because the triune God exists as a community of three persons, we reflect the image of God in our existence as social beings in community. Just as the three different members of the Trinity are bound together, and God and God's creation are bound together, so the different members of the human community are bound together. Therefore, the second limit to one's individual freedom and autonomy is respect for the autonomy and differences of one's neighbors. Our selfishness blinds us to the fact that free human agents are not fully human without others. Consequently, as Christians and as inhabitants of the planet, we are called to practice respect and solidarity for the sake of the common good and universal peace.

Respect Differences

What does it mean for us to value and respect the honor, dignity, and self-determination of individuals, congregations, denominations, other faiths, nations, secular organizations, and even our enemies? We might start by considering the questions our policy statement poses under the principle "Recognition and Respect":

- Is there recognition of the self-affirmed identities of each partner?
- Are the unique contexts of all partners recognized and respected?
- Are gifts and needs of all partners affirmed and respected?
- Are cultural differences being mediated with sincerity and in a Christ-like manner?[3]

To treat others as subjects/agents created in God's image is to respect their intrinsic qualities, gifts, and choices. "We have gifts that differ. . . ." (Rom. 12:6). Embodied and incarnate Christianity begins by respecting the physical characteristics and condition of every person. Moving beyond genetic qualities, we respect the personality, mental capacity, perceptions, opinions, feelings, and ideas of others. We respect the vocational, economic, and social location of individuals and groups. We welcome the challenges and questions of others' experiences, values, religious beliefs, economic systems, and political ideology. We learn to recognize and value difference rather than seeking to ignore, minimize, or eliminate it.

A challenge for privileged North Americans is learning to show respect for the race, ethnic identity, culture, and nationality of others. Especially in crosscultural settings, whether as hosts or as guests, mission partners must demonstrate respect for each other's culture. When we go as "strangers" to other countries, we need to learn something of the language, experiences, values, religious beliefs, and political ideology that form the metanarrative of our host culture. We will discover many things that seem strange to us. For strangers to become guests, they must accept and embody as fully as possible the values and customs of their host culture. Missionaries today must be careful not to repeat the errors of past mission work that forced Christians outside the North Atlantic to reject and abandon many of their own cultural traditions and imposed Western "civilization" upon them.

Showing Mutual Respect

In *every encounter* with every person, group, or culture, we demonstrate (usually unconsciously) authentic respect *or* disrespect. This includes the homeless or the beggar on the street, the student in the classroom, those who serve us and whom we serve, family, neighbors, colleagues, elected officials, church members, people of other nationalities and religions, and complete strangers. Regardless of whether we speak to or engage the other, we show an attitude either of respect or disrespect. Before we speak or act in mission partnerships, we must consciously and intentionally show respect. How?

1. *See, recognize, acknowledge, and turn to the other.* The problem with the rich man was that he was totally oblivious or indifferent to Lazarus "at his gate" (Luke 16:19–31). Thousands of people whose paths we cross daily are invisible or transparent to us. We simply ignore them or count them as unfocused objects in the background of life. It is extremely difficult to be sensitive and cognizant of every person we encounter each day; at the same time, it is very simple.

Each culture has ways of recognizing the presence of the other. In many cultures respect begins with eye contact that acknowledges the existence of the other. In some Asian cultures, initial eye contact shows a lack of respect. It is important to discover the correct way to recognize and acknowledge the existence and presence of the other. In Brazil when a person enters a room, that person greets every individual, whether friend or stranger, with a word, handshake, or kiss on the cheek. The same ritual is repeated upon leaving. When Brazilians come to the United States, they feel invisible when people one day greet them and the next day pass by them with no word or gesture of recognition.

If the church is serious about recognition and respect, then we are going to have to truly become mindful of the existence and feelings of others. It is a question of conscious awareness and exposure, of learning how to open ourselves up, of being willing to listen to the questions and challenges of others, of developing relationships of mutual give-and-take. As a result of this process, we will see the world with new eyes and gain new perspectives. We will comprehend both our culture and other cultures in a new light. We will discover that the view from the outside and especially from the underside is broader. Suddenly we may perceive that we have become global Christians and global citizens. This in turn leads us to a resistance of attitudes that are not respectful of all others.

2. *Make others feel they are human beings worthy of dignity and respect.* When partners engage in God's mission together, they should feel mutually respected as equals. Underlying attitudes of disrespect cause one partner to feel humiliated, discriminated, guilty, or exploited. We need to show people that we value them as subjects who are important and have something to give. Others are no longer just recipients; they are also partners who give and act. Respect takes seriously the contributions of all people. We must graciously accept the gifts people offer us and humbly learn the profound lessons of faith they teach us. Respect acknowledges the presence and potential of every person and enhances the dignity of all.

Behind the gifts, words, gestures, and hospitality that hosts extend to their honored guests is their expression of respect. It is vital to prepare oneself to receive respect from others, as they see fit to show it. Respect can be shown through body language, formal speech or titles, invitations to participate in worship services or cultural festivities, the offering of certain culinary delicacies, or by silence. We must be sensitive and humbly receive the respect offered us.

3. *Try to identify and be part of the agenda of others.* In order for our mission endeavors to truly be relevant and welcome, we must be careful to not take our political or ethical agenda to other countries and impose it on our partners. Likewise, we must not overwhelm partner churches with our initia-

tives, projects, resources, and priorities. Invitations and legitimation of outsiders only come through respect, never through force, awe, or fear. As guests in other countries, we go without agendas in order to discover the agendas of our partner churches. The first concern in a partnership is to get to know one another and cultivate relationships by observing, listening, and asking questions. We should make an intentional effort to find out all we can about every person we have the privilege of meeting and be prepared to hear English with accents different from our own. We must respect the culture, leadership, structures, projects, policy, planning, and priorities of our partners. It is for this reason that the PC(USA) strongly recommends that new partnerships refrain from any type of funding for two years.

I was graciously received by the Rev. Gloria Roja, president of the Evangelical Lutheran Church in Chile in her office in Santiago. She told of painful experiences of her denomination that had resulted from serious mistakes of mission workers, and her stories caused me to reflect on the complexities of partnerships. "Let's keep working at partnerships," she urged, "and get beyond money as the main issue. What we most need is recognition of our full dignity. Don't bring us your initiatives; come alongside us and join us in completing our initiatives."

The only way we can participate in change in other places is by identifying concerns on the agendas of our partners and then joining in solidarity with them as they express consternation, repudiate unjust actions, and seek social transformation in their own countries. Likewise, partners who come to our country can join us in our resistance to sinful structures and in other mission priorities we have.

Respectful Disagreement or Disapproval

To respect is not necessarily to agree. While we have the obligation to respect others, we have the freedom to disagree with their ideas and actions. Furthermore, we can radically disapprove of the choices of others. We respect people and debate ideas. There is absolutely no problem in protesting again the positions of others, as long as we do it respectfully.

Some examples might be helpful. While we recognize the legitimacy and respect the faiths of other people, without reticence we can humbly share our faith commitment to Jesus Christ as Lord and Savior. In evangelistic opportunities, we should articulate our beliefs in a friendly, positive manner and respect those who do not agree or embrace the gospel as we understand it. Respect allows us to engage both in witness and dialogue with people of different religions and people of no professed religion. Additionally, when we affirm others' rights to their faith, we can work together as neighbors and citizens around common tasks and goals for a world of justice, peace, and love. This is the ideal and purpose of the United Nations and the World Council of Churches. Respectful attitudes enable us to live peaceably and to seek responsible life in community. Protestant, Catholic, and Orthodox Christians disagree on certain doctrines and practices, but we act and dialogue in ecumenical partnerships with mutual respect.

In some instances, not only do we disagree with the ideas and positions of others, but we blatantly disapprove and denounce their actions and values. It is possible to disapprove and disagree with the ideas and positions of others and prophetically denounce their actions and values with respect. We witnessed this in 2003 in the demonstrations for peace in the United States and around the world. The PC(USA) is engaged in such a dialogue and disagreement around issues of sexuality and ordination. In ethical and political debates, when we find ourselves in radical opposition to certain interpretations and actions, we must respectfully listen to and seek to understand the other's decision or position and also express our own. Respectful disagreement over an issue does not have to end friendships or destroy communities and alliances.

Continuing Conversion toward Respect

Mission involves a dynamic interaction of differences for the sake of mutual transformation and mutual conversion. Christ transforms cultures and persons. God wants to transform us and renew God's image in us so that we can participate in God's mission on our journey toward the fullness of God's reign. Because God respects our free will and does not aggressively impose transformation, the pathway of partnership in mission involves our consent, openness, vulnerability, discipline, self-critique, and continuing conversion. If God seeks to show one culture a better way through exposure to another culture, it is best to wait until both come to know each other extremely well before presuming to know what it is that God wants to change. In *The Continuing Conversion of the Church,* Darrell L. Guder envisions the conversion of the mission worker, the local congregation, and the institutional church. He says, *"Mission is to be a continuing process of translation and witness, whereby the evangelist and the mission community will discover again and again that they will be confronted by the gospel as it is translated, heard, and responded to, and will thus experience ongoing conversion while serving as witness"* (italics in the original).[4]

How is the gospel confronting and converting us in our mission work today? Where have we failed? Where are we lacking? We from the United States silently suffer the bitter consequences of our unintentional "culture of discrimination" and attitude of condescension, which often disrespects, denigrates, blames, ignores, and alienates others. Because our complicity is unintentional and deeply rooted in our culture and church, it is naturally disguised to us. In other words, we think and assume that as well-meaning Christians and law-abiding citizens we are respectful of others. We are unaware of how disrespectful we can be in our language, attitudes, and actions without even noticing it. I only discovered this and initiated my "continual conversion toward respect" when Brazilians and people of other nationalities who were treated in disrespectful ways by Anglo-Americans trusted me enough to share their painful experiences.

Joerg Rieger suggests that the "turn to others" starts with a *critique*, "Clearly, a more self-critical perspective is needed. Exclusive structures, especially where they are pursued on unconscious levels, cannot be challenged by merely admitting our fallibility and by claiming more inclusivity. Self-critique in the true sense of the word is only possible where the self gains an outside perspective on itself."[5] I experienced this as I followed the war in Iraq from Brazil.

Attitudes of superiority and arrogance that breed disrespect and indifference are a part of our Western cultural heritage, and they foment strong negative feelings of other nations against the United States. This contributed to the anger behind the horrendous terrorist attacks on New York City and Washington, D.C. on September 11, 2001. The world responded with acts of solidarity towards our wounded nation. It was an opportunity to recognize our need for the help of others and to join hands with nations around the world in the fight against global terrorism. Unfortunately, we lost this opportunity and were swept up by fear and an exacerbated nationalism and chose the path of unilateralism rather than interdependence. The unilateral U.S. intervention in Iraq without the support of the United Nations alienated old allies and ignited a new wave of intense anti-Americanism around the globe. The predicted rift between the civilizations and religions of East and West has become a reality.

As we seek reorientation for mission, the time is ripe to courageously heed Rieger's words: "The primary issue is not first of all advocacy, in the form of doing things for others in ways that leave the self intact, but self-critique."[6] Mission in Christ's way does not demean or humiliate anyone with charitable handouts and impersonal disrespectful treatment. It is anti-gospel to offer material assistance at home or abroad without respecting the dignity of others and entering into authentic caring mutual relationships. God's holistic mission is based on respect, risk, and trust.

God's Spirit, who sends, guides, corrects, and continually converts us as we participate in *missio Dei,* will surely help us to recognize, name, own, and confess where we have erred in our missional attitudes and practices. We must engage our blind spots and actively resist attitudes and structures of disrespect. The road to mission in partnership includes repentance of our wrong and misguided attitudes, even though they are unintentional or cultural.

Repentance, however, is much more than feeling bad about our mostly unconscious lack of respect. It is a self-critique that leads to thinking, acting, seeing, and treating others differently. The challenge before us today is to honor the image of God in ourselves and in our neighbor and, as we engage in mission partnerships, to approach every person, congregation, denomination, nation, and organization with intentional respect.

Chapter 4

Missional Attitudes: Compassion

Out of the believer's heart shall flow rivers of living water.
—John 7:38

When Jesus saw [Mary] weeping, and the Jews who came with her also weeping, he was greatly disturbed in spirit and deeply moved. He said, "Where have you laid [Lazarus]?" They said to him, "Lord, come and see." Jesus began to weep. So the Jews said, "See how he loved him!"
—John 11:33–36

*T*hroughout the Hebrew Scriptures we perceive that God hears the cries of the afflicted and responds to human suffering with love, compassion, and mercy. God feels and shares the suffering of God's creatures and creation. In the incarnation Jesus identifies with the broken world and finally suffers on the cross. Jesus' response to the pain, suffering, grief, and death of others is profoundly emotional. Jesus shows us what it means to be truly human, a whole person. Jesus has the courage to sense, face, and share another's pain and to weep publicly. The Synoptic Gospels (Matthew, Mark, and Luke) use the verb "to have compassion" to describe Jesus' missional attitude in response to need and suffering. When the two blind men cried out, "Lord, have mercy," and expressed their need, "moved with compassion, Jesus touched their eyes" (Matt. 20:34). When Lazarus died, Jesus wept, sharing the anguish and grief of his sisters and brothers. Compassion is feeling, touching, and weeping. It is standing in solidarity with society's victims.

Flowing from Our Inner Being

Compassion is the English translation of a very interesting Greek word (*splangkhnidzomahee*) used in the New Testament that is as hard for us to pronounce as it is to practice. The root meaning is "inward parts," or entrails, which describes the seat of the emotions that grips the whole personality at the most profound level. Compassion is a strong feeling, sensibility, or attitude of love and affection, a visceral reaction at the "gut level" or depths of one's emotional being that moves one to embrace the pathos or painful situation of another. Compassion is the inner spirit that motivates, shapes, and accompanies our response to the world's needs. It is embodied hurt that involves both love and pain, as does childbirth. Kristine Haig, PC(USA) spiritual director, says, "Compassion means 'to suffer with'—not merely to notice someone else's pain and feel sorry for them, but to share in that very pain and feel it in our own being."[1]

Compassion or mercy is the visceral source that stand behind, the emotional motor that propels, the sensitive spirit that accompanies the practice of God's mission. It is one thing to limit ourselves to the mere practice of "works of mercy" or to engage dutifully in "ministries of compassion," and another thing to be moved by the "attitude of compassion." For this reason, *"being" or attitudes must undergird all partner relationships and missional practices together.* The Fourth Gospel tells us that the "rivers of living water" that Jesus promised would flow "out of the believer's heart" (literally belly) refer to the Holy Spirit (John 7:38–39). John teaches us that the Spirit "abides" in us, in our inner being. Because of the Spirit at work in us, compassion—as our *reaction* to the need of the other—flows out of our being and involves our heart, hands, feet, and head—the whole person. Before we can exercise compassion, we must experience God's compassion and allow it to move and control our whole being, to flow forth from our inner self. Because of God's compassion toward us, God forgives and renews us. Our response is to love and worship God with our hearts, souls, minds, and all of our physical being and to love our neighbors as ourselves. If we open and yield ourselves, the Holy Spirit enables us in worship and in mission with all of God's children to become a compassionate community in service to the world. The PC(USA) Directory for Worship says,

> Following the example of Jesus Christ, faithful disciples today express compassion
> a. with respect for the dignity of those in need,
> b. with openness to help even those judged undeserving,
> c. with willingness to risk their own comfort and safety,
> d. with readiness to receive as well as to give,
> e. with constant prayer in the midst of ministering, always in communion with the renewing power of the worshiping community.[2]

An Emotional Re-action

Jesus' relationship with God and with others and all of his missional actions were molded and bathed by what I call the "attitude of compassion" or what Jon Sobrino calls "the principle of mercy." He says, "By the principle of mercy, we understand here a specific love, which, while standing at the origin of a process, also remains present and active throughout the process, endowing it with a particular direction and shaping the various elements that compose it. We hold that this principle of mercy is the basic principle of the activity of God and Jesus, and therefore ought to be that of the activity of the church."[3]

The attitude of compassion or the principle of mercy was the essence of Jesus' inner being, which spontaneously produced an emotional *re-action* to human need. This affective re-action, which we call compassion, shaped his entire life and mission. Jesus' response to the suffering and sin of the world was always *com*-passion. Matthew uses the story of the healing of the blind men outside Jericho as a conclusion to the public ministry of Jesus and an introduction to his passion. When Jesus and his disciples were leaving Jericho, two blind men sitting by the roadside shouted, " 'Lord, have mercy on us, Son of David!' " Jesus saw and heard them over the tumult and asked a question that empowered them to identify their own need, " 'What do you want me to do for you?' " They said to him, " 'Lord, let our eyes be opened.' " What was Jesus' re-action? How did Jesus respond? "Moved with compassion, Jesus touched their eyes." It was an emotional response that emanated from his inner being and involved his body. Sensing their pain, "Jesus touched their eyes. Immediately they regained their sight and followed him" (Matt. 20:29–34).

The compassion of "the Lamb of God who takes away the sin of the world" (John 1:29) reached a climax of embodied passion at Calvary. Jesus took on our suffering in his body. Even in his most agonizing moment on the cross, Jesus reacted to the despair of others with compassion. "When Jesus saw his mother and the disciple whom he loved standing beside her, he said to his mother, 'Woman, here is your son.' Then he said to the disciple, 'Here is your mother' " (John 19:26–27).

Latin Americans are emotional, highly sensitive to the needs of the other, and spontaneously moved to compassion and acts of solidarity. Let me give you some examples. After a terrible flash flood in Brazil, I saw a very poor woman on the news whose shack was spared, along with two beds, hers and her daughter's. As a compassionate human being, she thankfully said, "I have

an abundance and want to give one bed to my neighbor who lost everything."
Compassion moves people to give sacrificially in response to human need.

I know a Brazilian seamstress whose natural response to all suffering is
compassion. The evening world news often brings her to tears and robs her of
sleep. She told me that one day she was walking down the street and saw a
construction worker with a strip of bad sunburn where his shirt was torn.
Moved with compassion, she went home with tears in her eyes, brought one
of her son's shirts to the man, took his torn shirt home, washed and tenderly
mended it, and returned it to him. This is compassion. What is the state of my
compassionate friend's "inward parts"? I see in her attitude the freedom to
feel and to let her feelings show, the urgency of emotion, a heightened sensitivity to the feelings of others, a readiness to change her day's plan in the face
of human need, and an openness to care for others.

As a European American who was not socialized to feel and demonstrate
my emotions, I have discovered the nature and texture of the attitude of compassion by living in the Latin American culture. European Americans tend to
rely more on reason. Those who have abundant material resources often
respond to human need by writing a check. No empathy or emotion is
involved, only responsibility and maybe guilt. All of us have much to learn
from the worldwide church. Compassion is not feeling sorry for or feeling
responsible for others. It is interiorizing their pain. Only then are we ready to
respond with authentic missional practices. A Nigerian Presbyterian pastor in
one of my classes said that service or aid that is not compassionate is not even
humanitarian. It can be cold and calculating. Mission actions with good intentions and wrong attitudes are questionable.

An Open Heart

Jesus had compassion. In Mark 6 Jesus calls the twelve disciples and sends
them out two by two in mission (6:7–13). In verse 30 Mark tells of the debriefing of the apostles after their missionary excursion. The plan is to get away
from the pressing demands and retreat for rest and sharing. The problem is
that the crowds get wind of the schema and are there waiting when they arrive.
What does Jesus do? How does he react to the intruding multitude?

Mark's account (6:30–44) contains a highly significant pattern that shapes
Jesus' mission practice: Jesus "saw a great crowd; and he had compassion for
them, because they were like sheep without a shepherd" (Mark 6:34). Openness is the state of being that gave Jesus the flexibility to be interrupted, to
change his plans, and to sacrificially see beyond his own needs and those of

openness (margin annotation)

his disciples to see the needs of the crowd. Mission begins with openness to God's Spirit and to others. Respect means that we truly see others. Compassion means that we are truly open to feel the pain of others. To "be open" is an explosive mission term. Openness can lead to a compassionate response. Because Jesus respects the crowd, he sees them. Because Jesus is open to the crowd, he gives up control and his personal plans in order to respond to their needs. Compassion is the opposite of control. We can be compassionate only to the degree that we are willing to let go and respond with sensitivity to the suffering of the other. Jesus saw beyond the immediate requests and discerned their deep need for meaning, purpose, and direction.

Jesus' compassion envelopes the whole person and the whole range of suffering humanity. He finishes teaching and immediately faces another challenge. What do you do when everyone is hungry and you have nothing to eat? The disciples' suggestion is to forget about compassion and send the crowd away to fend for themselves. No, Jesus says, "You give them something to eat" (Mark 6:37). The disciples, like many Christians in the West, naturally think in terms of budgetary cost and one-way mission "out of affluence." Jesus follows another model based on sharing of local resources: "How many loaves have you? Go and see" (Mark 6:38). Jesus values and gladly receives a child's meager gift of five loaves and two fish. He breaks the bread and shares it with the community. The child becomes a partner in God's holistic mission. Only shared bread will feed the world. If the church's mission of providing material assistance to others is not marked by a sense of openness to the other's pain, or compassion, it is not God's mission.

Out of Vulnerability

Matthew's introduction to the missionary sending of the twelve disciples (Matt. 9:35–38) includes the repeated pattern: "When [Jesus] *saw* the crowds, he *had compassion* for them, because they were harassed and helpless, like sheep without a shepherd" (Matt. 9:36; italics added). Jesus' compassion arises from a respectful and perceptive awareness of their situation. Jesus saw them not as passive objects or numbers, but as human beings who suffer injustices and deceptions that threaten their self-dignity.

Opening ourselves to the world's needs and pains is overwhelming. When we vulnerably internalize and embody the helplessness of others, we feel helpless and even paralyzed. What do we do with the pain? Jesus wept and prayed over Jerusalem. Jesus' life had a rhythm of contemplative prayer and compassionate service. Immediately after sensing the crowd's agony, Jesus said to his disciples, "'The harvest is plentiful, but the laborers are few; therefore ask the Lord of the harvest to send out laborers into [God's] harvest'" (Matt. 9:37, 38). In John 4:35 Jesus told the disciples to "'see how the fields are ripe for harvesting.'" Sometimes all we can see is suffering and violence. Nonetheless, the triune missionary God is at work in the world establishing God's reign of peace and justice, gathering for God's future. To be a "laborer" in God's harvest is to face the pain within ourselves and in others with hope and to pray, "'Your kingdom come'" (Matt. 6:10).

God's answer to our prayers for the world often involves us. Matthew then tells us that the twelve were commissioned and *sent out* with missional instructions (Matt. 10:1–5). Among them is the statement "'See, I am sending you out like sheep into the midst of wolves; so be wise as serpents and innocent as doves'" (Matt. 10:16). We observed in John's Gospel that although disciples become shepherds who feed sheep, they never cease to be sheep. This idea is reinforced in Matthew. Though we see others as "harassed and helpless, like sheep without a shepherd" (Matt. 9:36), we too go out in mission "like sheep," not as wolves or lions. Gentle lambs are models for building respectful relationships with people of other cultures and races. Isaiah's Suffering Servant is an image worthy of our contemplation as North Americans: "He was oppressed, and he was afflicted, yet he did not open his mouth; like a lamb that is led to the slaughter, and like a sheep that before its shearers is silent, so he did not open his mouth" (Isa. 53:7).

In the twenty-first century, if we go out in mission with attitudes of superiority and arrogance, no one will accept us. If we think that mission is using our abundant financial resources and exhibiting our technological advances, we are in for a rude awakening. We must follow Christ in mission as "sheep," aware of our fragility, vulnerability, and tendency to stray. We engage in mission not as "messiahs" or "conquerors" but as human beings in solidarity with all other human beings. We must learn to do mission out of our cultural, emotional, and spiritual poverty, rather than out of our material abundance. As "sheep" we first must recognize our own pain and helplessness, our own need for the help of others, our own feelings, and our own limitations. We open ourselves to receive the compassion of others in mutual partnerships. Only from this posture of weakness, need, and vulnerability can compassion flow from our inward being.

Touching Wounds

Jesus taught compassion. The verb "to have compassion" that characterizes Jesus' missional attitude is used in the Lukan parables of the Good Samaritan and the Prodigal Son to connote a specific human attitude or emotional response to the need of others, based on the extravagant compassion of our divine Parent.

After sending the twelve disciples on a missionary journey in Luke 9, Jesus appoints and sends seventy mission volunteers in the tenth chapter. Jesus' insistence on sending "pairs" reminds us that mission is done in partnerships. The increasing numbers participating in God's mission remind us that the entire church is sent. Jesus gives them instructions about vulnerability and dependency on the hospitality of their hosts, "eating and drinking whatever they provide" (Luke 10:7). It is clear that mission partnerships involve intimate table fellowship and personal interaction.

Luke then recounts the joyful return and debriefing of the seventy. We see how important it is for all involved in mission to have an opportunity to report to their local congregations and presbyteries. We must share all the marvelous things God is doing in mission. While Jesus does not discourage their enthusiasm, he gently corrects their misplaced sensationalism and leads them to a more correct theological vision (Luke 10:17–20). Groups returning from mission trips today also need this kind of critical evaluation.

Again Jesus' conversation with his disciples is interrupted, this time by an opponent. In his answer to the proud lawyer's question, "And who is my neighbor?", Jesus respectfully pushes cultural boundaries, imagines role reversals, and challenges stereotypes. His story makes the rejected Samaritan the hero who follows Jesus' model of compassionate mission service (Luke 10:25–37). Walter Brueggemann reminds us that

> Jesus in his solidarity with the marginal ones is *moved to compassion* (italics in the original). Compassion constitutes a radical form of criticism, for it announces that the hurt is to be taken seriously, that the hurt is not to be accepted as normal and natural but is an abnormal and unacceptable condition for humanness. . . . Thus the compassion of Jesus is to be understood not simply as a personal emotional reaction but as a public criticism in which he dares to act upon his concern against the entire numbness of his social context.[4]

The criticism in this parable is blatant. Both religious leaders in the story *saw* the wounded man, but they continued their journey. Seeing is not enough. Did they really *see* him? Does the church today really see our wounded neighbors along the road and recognize our complicity in their pain? When the passing Samaritan "saw him, he was moved with pity [compassion]. He went to him and bandaged his wounds, having poured oil and wine on them" (Luke 10:33–34). He compassionately *re*-acted from his inner being to the other's pain and *inter*-acted with the man. This meant tenderly touching and caring for his wounds. However, his mission service was not merely "hit-or-miss" "band-aids" from an isolated outsider. He sought medical help (a local partner in mission) and committed himself to sustained treatment.

Jesus teaches the argumentative religious lawyer that Christian doctrine is based on the missional attitude of being open, as the Samaritan is open, fearlessly crossing cultural boundaries and touching ugly wounds. "Go and do likewise" (Luke 10:37). Learn from the Samaritan. Imitate the Samaritan. Let your heart of stone be turned into a heart of flesh. Allow the other's pain to move you to compassion. Be a compassionate neighbor to all who are in pain, to the suffering, rejected, and marginalized people in the ditches of life. Today those in the dominant culture must experience "mission-in-reverse" and learn about compassion from the poor and disenfranchised. I have learned more from my Brazilian, Mexican, African, and Asian students and friends than I have ever taught them.

Being Embraced and Embracing

In the parable of the Prodigal Son who repents and returns home (Luke 15:11–32), we find a wonderful description of God's compassionate heart. We see the recurrent pattern: "But while he was still far off, his father saw him and was filled with compassion; he ran and put his arms around him and kissed him" (15:20). Have you ever wondered how the father happened to be attentively gazing at the horizon the day his son returned and what the father's days were like while he was away? Were they long days of silent affliction, deep pain, and hopeful waiting? We know that God forces nobody, respects human autonomy, and allows God's children to make wrong choices and suffer the consequences. God also suffers because of our wrong choices that result in violence and injustice in the world. God patiently waits and agonizes over the pain our sin causes. God never gives up or loses hope. A waiting God. A long-suffering God. A God of hope.

Like the prodigal child in Luke's parable, we have sinned against God and others, and must seek, as did the prodigal, forgiveness and reconciliation. A basic problem for the church in the United States today is that our affluence causes us sometimes to make wasteful expenditures and practice "works of compassion" with an attitude of pride. In the process of administering our resources, there has been "a not-so-subtle shift" in which "compassion and solidarity" have been "replaced by pity and condescension."[5] In other words, our superiority, guilt, and egocentrism structure and mold our response to the world's needs. The global community resents and rejects our abundant resources, which have caused much destruction and unpayable foreign debts. We face an unprecedented crisis of credibility. Nations are enraged by our aid or mission work offered without compassion and in complicity with imperialism. It is costly for the church or any institution to react with compassion and maintain an attitude of compassion over self-centeredness. It requires a continuing conversion toward compassion.

As North Americans, we must "come to ourselves" and humbly admit to the non-Western world, we "have sinned against heaven and before you" and are "no longer worthy to be called" mission partners (Luke 15:21). We live in a world of both sin and grace. My suspicion is that our partner churches will be as compassionate and forgiving as the Father in the parable.

How does the waiting Parent respond when his filthy, ragged, rebellious son appears on the horizon? Compassion takes over. Compassion compels the dignified Mid-Eastern patriarch to run. The intense emotional response is embodied and relational. No questions. No lessons to teach. No conditions. No problem solving. No analysis. No ceremony. No formality. No emotional distance and restraint. No barriers. It is the amazing miracle and mystery of God's incarnate love toward us. God's compassion is unconditional and extravagant. It wells up inside of one's being and overflows with feelings, tears, touch, and embrace. The joyful festival that follows demonstrates mission as forgiveness, reconciled relationship, and celebration.

In one of the plenary addresses of the Eighth Assembly of the World Council of Churches in Harare (1998), theologian Kosuke Koyama used this parable to affirm that "God is a running God." Ofelia Ortega, President of the Seminario Evangélico de Teología in Matanzas, Cuba, comments, "God runs from the centre to the periphery (Luke 15:20), thus transforming the periphery into centre. God turns the invisible into visible when he urges 'Quickly, bring out a robe—the best one—and put it on him; put a ring on his finger and sandals on his feet. And get the fatted calf. . . .'"[6] In the joyful reunion, the son is treated with respect and compassion, and dignity is restored.

Marian McClure links Koyama's image to "Pentecost and the response to God's compassion." She perceptively says, "The sound of the rushing wind at Pentecost is the sound of God rushing toward us in extravagant love. Our response in mission is to live gratefully, offering the world freely the compassion and generosity we have received through Christ without meriting it." McClure further remarks, "As at Pentecost, our experience of God having run toward us in compassion, immediately becomes an occasion for our own running toward the world in compassion" and exhorts us to a "constant running, running, running toward the world in compassion."[7]

In order for us to run toward others in compassion, we have to open our hearts to become conduits for God's Spirit. Participation in God's mission from a position of vulnerability and weakness involves heart first, then running feet, embracing arms, and transforming minds. When our global response to the suffering world is structured by sinful attitudes that block God's compassion from flowing into and through our lives, we are not doing God's mission. God wants to embrace us and enable us to run in compassion to receive and give embraces. May the balm of God's healing and gratuitous embrace penetrate and renew our "inward parts" and cause to well up in us a compassionate emotional re-action to the pain and wounds around us.

Chapter 5

Missional Attitudes: Humility

Jesus . . . got up from the table, took off his outer robe, and tied a towel around himself. Then he poured water into a basin and began to wash the disciples' feet and to wipe them with the towel that was tied around him. . . . After he had washed their feet, had put on his robe, and had returned to the table, he said to them, "Do you know what I have done to you? You call me Teacher and Lord—and you are right, for that is what I am. So if I, your Lord and Teacher, have washed your feet, you also ought to wash one another's feet. For I have set you an example, that you also should do as I have done to you."

—John 13:3–5, 12–15

*J*esus Christ not only completed the unique saving mission for which God sent him into the world, but also was a model of humility for the church sent in the power of the Spirit. The Fourth Gospel uses the terms "coming" and "going" in reference to Jesus' descent and ascent. While these terms testify to Jesus' divine origin, "coming into the world" (John 1:9; 3:19; 9:39; 12:46; 16:28; and 18:37) was also an act of humility. In the incarnation the coeternal creative "Word became flesh and lived among us" (John 1:14). Jesus' baptism was a solidarity plunge of humility (John 1:29–34). Though the cross in the Fourth Gospel is seen more as the path to glorification and "mission completed" by being "lifted up" in order to "draw all people to [himself]" (John 12:32), at Golgotha Jesus "humbled himself" and also was humiliated by others. The images of Jesus "carrying the cross by himself" (John 19:17), being crucified between two common criminals, crying out, "I am thirsty" and "It is finished," then bowing his head and giving up his spirit (John 19:28, 30), demonstrate the emotional depths of Jesus' descent to the human condition.

The washing of the disciples' feet is strategically placed as a preface to

Jesus' Farewell Discourse in John 14–16. In an intimate setting of table fellowship Jesus wants to impress upon those who will soon be sent that partnership in God's mission is sharing in love. Mission is self-emptying, self-giving, and other-receiving. The only way to follow Jesus is with a humble spirit.

Sharing Grace

How does a person engaged in mission follow Jesus' "example, that you also should do as I have done to you" (John 13:15)? Saul of Tarsus, a proud well-educated Pharisee, who had every reason to boast (see Phil. 3:4–6), became Paul, the humble servant of Jesus Christ. A radical and continual transformation stirred Paul's inner spirit and marked his way of living. The attitudes that flowed from the inner being of this pioneer missionary are instructive for us.

The first church that Paul and his coworkers founded in Europe was in Philippi (according to Acts 16). Paul moved on to other mission work and was in prison for preaching the gospel. While there, he received a monetary gift and news from the church (Phil. 4:18). Paul had a very special relationship with this church that was his partner in God's mission. He writes a letter of gratitude to them with thanks to God for their "partnership" or "fellowship" or "sharing in the gospel" (Phil. 1:5). The Greek word he uses, *koinonia,* basically means "partaking together in" a group. It can be translated partnership, fellowship, communion, participation, or sharing. *Koinonia* is sharing in community, participating in community. A palpable expression of it is seen in meaningful common meals. Andrew Kirk says, "Perhaps the nearest word in the New Testament to partnership is *koinonia,*" which can include sharing in a common project, sharing of gifts, sharing of material resources, and/or sharing in suffering.[1] Paul and the Philippians participated in a partnership in many ways. They were partners in giving, receiving, working, praying, rejoicing, struggling, and suffering. Partnership is a relationship. To be "partners in the gospel" is to be partners with God and all of God's people in fellowship and mission.

It was their vital mutual partnership that led Paul to make this strong affective statement: "It is right for me to think this way about all of you, because you hold me in your heart, for all of you *share in God's grace* with me, both in my imprisonment and in the defense and confirmation of the gospel. For God is my witness, how I long for all of you with the compassion of Christ Jesus" (Phil. 1:7–8; italics added). The word for "share" is a cognate of *koinonia.* Mission in partnership is sharing grace and compassion as joint heirs. Jesus told Peter, "'Unless I wash you, you have no share with me'"

(John 13:8). To participate in the triune mission community means that our "heritage" is to share in God's love, life, mission, and grace.

Sharing grace gives partners the courage to engage in honest self-critique, confession, and correction. Paul's tender words of gratitude to the Philippian faith community, coupled with his bold exhortation, help us to understand and implement one of the principles of partnership in the PC(USA) policy statement:

> *Shared Grace and Thanksgiving.* Partnership *calls* all partners to confess individual and collective failings, to seek forgiveness for complicity with powers of injustice, to repent from histories of shared exploitation, to move toward common celebration of Christ's sacrifice of reconciliation, and together to give thanks and praise to God for all gifts of grace and renewal.[2]

Evidently, some serious relational and attitudinal problems have disturbed the harmony, unity, and, consequently, the witness of the Philippian church. Paul bases his exhortation on their shared experiences of grace and deep-felt mission partnership: "If then there is any encouragement in Christ, any consolation from love, any sharing in the Spirit, any compassion and sympathy, make my joy complete . . ." (Phil. 2:1–2a). Because of God's missional action, the believing community at Philippi have all shared in the encouraging, consoling, compassionate love and grace of the triune God. Paul firmly shows them the key to all relationships in the body of Christ: "Be of the same mind, having the same love, being in full accord and of one mind" (Phil. 2:2b). The pivotal word "mind" (2:2, 5) does not refer to doctrine or signify constant agreement. It means to have a common attitude or orientation, a certain way of thinking and being, a mind-set, "an approach to life, to others, to self, to God which characterizes those who are in Christ Jesus."[3] What attitude is this? What way of being or spirituality marks the totality of life in Christ?

> Let the same mind be in you that was in Christ Jesus,
>   who, though he was in the form of God,
>   did not regard equality with God
>   as something to be exploited,
>   but emptied himself,
>   taking the form of a slave,
>   being born in human likeness.
>   And being found in human form,
>   he humbled himself
>   and became obedient to the point of death—
>   even death on a cross.
>   —Phil. 2:5–8

Paul inspires his partner church in Philippi to imitate the "mind" or "attitude" of Christ. The ancient liturgical piece that Paul cites (Phil. 2:6–11) poignantly reminds us that in his incarnation and in his death our Lord "humbled himself."

Letting Go of Entitlement and Privilege

It is noteworthy that the verb is reflexive; Jesus humbled *himself;* he is both the autonomous subject and the object of the action. It is a conscious practice that the self chooses to effect on its self. Only Christ could humble himself. When the subject and object are different, it is humiliation. Humility is the attitude we should have toward ourselves. We must humble ourselves and never humiliate others. All disrespect toward others is humiliation. Jesus "humbled himself" and also was humiliated by others.

How did Christ humble himself? Rather than clinging to his entitled rights and privileges as God, he "emptied himself" in order to assume the vulnerabilities of human existence. Claude Labrunie of the United Presbyterian Church of Brazil explains: "The Letter to the Philippians sought a word to express this mysterious action whereby God extends his hand, and it found the word 'emptiness': God emptied himself, became poor, in solidarity with the poor because he was poor himself. If he became empty he lost his autonomy, his independence. God had to make himself a poor person."[4] God freely limited God's absolute freedom. Jürgen Moltmann, in his book *The Trinity and the Kingdom,* says that the *kenosis* or self-humiliation of God began with creation, is "fulfilled in the incarnation of the Son" when the "triune God enters into the limited, finite situation," and is "completed and perfected in the passion and death of Jesus the Son."[5]

Along these lines, in 1964 the United Presbyterian Church in the United States of America (predecessor of the PC[USA]) approved a position paper that stated, "Partnership in Mission presupposes two or more autonomous church bodies which voluntarily limit their own independent action in missionary outreach in order to insure a mutually satisfactory and a more highly productive interdependence in missionary endeavor."[6] To limit our autonomy in order to respect the autonomy of the other, we must hold loosely any notion of entitlement and privilege.

Self-emptying

The incarnation presupposes the attitude of divine humility. Consequently, congregations are called to participate in God's mission with an attitude of humility. The PC(USA) policy statement says, "Guided by Christ's humility, we work to empty ourselves of all pride, power, sin, and privilege so that God may be glorified (Phil. 2:5–11)." Only through self-emptying can we begin to humble ourselves and let go of entitlement. To do mission in Jesus Christ's way, we seek to empty ourselves of the images of self-sufficient givers and dominant leaders. We seek to empty ourselves of the pride and excessive ethnocentrism associated with the all-too-common feelings of cultural, religious, or technological superiority that often grip us and blind us. We seek to empty ourselves of the need to initiate, control, impose, manipulate, and run ahead in partner relationships. We seek to empty ourselves of autonomy and independence in order to seek mutuality and reciprocity. Self-emptying is allowing our being to be filled with God and not with inflated ideas of ourselves. Our reflexive self-emptying before God is a kind of downward mobility that characterizes who we are and all we do in mission. Jesus described this downward mobility with these words: " 'Those who love their life lose it, and those who hate their life in this world will keep it for eternal life' " (John 12:25).

Why is it so difficult and rare for us to practice missional actions with humility? We in the United States of America are a very proud people. Our inheritance is a deeply ingrained sense of national pride. There is nothing necessarily wrong with that. The problem is the superiority complex and spirit of domination that have become part of our culture and collective consciousness. The Puritans believed that America was a place for God's elect people to be a shining example and a leader of democracy for the rest of the world. This nationalistic understanding led to the political doctrine of Manifest Destiny, which contends that the United States is destined by God to fulfill this political mission worldwide. Through the years our sense of "evangelical" responsibility has been tainted by pride and has developed into an offensive hegemony with arrogant imperialistic assumptions about our unique leadership role in the world.

Furthermore, according to missiologist David Bosch, during the past three centuries, the Enlightenment or "modern" era in the North Atlantic,

> together with the scientific and technological advances that followed in its wake, put the West at an unparalleled advantage over the rest of the world. Suddenly a limited number of nations had at their disposal "tools" and know-how vastly superior to those of others. The West could thus establish itself as master of all others in virtually every field. It was only logical that this feeling of superiority would also rub off on the "religion of the West", Christianity. As a matter of fact, in most cases there was no attempt to distinguish between religious and cultural supremacy—what applied to the one, applied equally axiomatically to the other.[7]

Clearly, we inheritors of the Enlightenment do have a problem with pride. Most of the world feels anger and resentment toward Anglo-Americans for actions and policies that reflect our imperialism and attitudes of superiority. This partially explains, though in no way justifies, the barbarous terrorist attacks on the World Trade Center and Pentagon on September 11, 2001. We rightfully denounced these acts of inhumane humiliation and rose from the dust with our dignity as human beings and citizens. However, rather than emptying ourselves of self-sufficiency and taking advantage of our moment of vulnerability to join hands with the interdependent world community in the search for justice and peace with no intent to further humiliate anyone, our uncritical vengeful nationalism led us down the path of proud unilateralism both in the war and reconstruction of Iraq. Many of our partner churches wrote to express pastoral caring but also dismay about the policy directions our country took in the aftermath. (See case study number 3, pp. 111–12.) Fortunately, President George W. Bush heeded Pope John Paul II's plea to not claim that our aggression was done with moral justification or in God's name.

Opposing Pride

James solemnly reminds us that "[God] gives all the more grace; therefore [Scripture] says, 'God opposes the proud, but gives grace to the humble'" (James 4:6). As a nation, as a church, and as North Americans it behooves us to humble ourselves. For this reason, the words in the PC(USA) document *Mission in the 1990s* ring forth with urgent relevance:

> [T]he style of mission as part of a global church can and must change. It must not be one of arrogance or domination but one of humility and repentance. It must be one of partnership and mutuality with the worldwide body of Christ. Our submission as Presbyterians to the principalities and powers that drive our culture and dominate our world is massive. We have fallen woefully short of bringing the Gospel mandate to bear in effective ways on this world. Repentance and obedience must be the beginning point for mission in the way of Christ who redeemed the world through his suffering love for all humanity.[8]

Furthermore, James instructs us, "Humble yourselves before the Lord" (4:10). As in Philippians 2:8, the verb "humble yourselves" is reflexive, an action that we consciously choose and practice on ourselves. In James 4:1–12 we discover that humility is the only appropriate attitude with which we can approach the Lord, and that it should be present also in our human relationships. Coherence requires that we treat others and the divine Other with love, respect, and humility. If we demonstrate superior disrespectful attitudes toward persons, cultures, or religions who are different, we are in the company of the Pharisee who said, " 'God, I thank you that I am not like other people' " (Luke 18:11). The only way we can go anywhere as missionaries today is with the words of the tax collector on our lips: " 'God, be merciful to me, a sinner!' " (Luke 18:13). Humility involves seeking mercy, yes, for it recognizes one's own sinful nature. How important it is in our relationship with God and with others to be ever aware of the fact that we are and always will be sinners in need of God's grace and forgiveness.

To humble oneself is not self-debasement or self-flagellation. We follow the example of Jesus and voluntarily humble ourselves as subjects with dignity worthy of the respect of others. It is to assume a posture of vulnerability and openness to the critical reflections of others, to admit our weaknesses and failures, and to practice honest self-critique and continuing conversion.

God calls us to personal humility in which we humble ourselves individually in our practice of mission and to collective national or congregational humility in which we help our church humble itself in its collective mission practice. We from the North Atlantic cannot turn a deaf ear to the costly lessons of history. We must truly humble ourselves, demonstrate fruits of repentance, and leave behind all attitudes of pride in mission. Collective humility, of a voluntary and self-imposed nature, is the antidote to colonialism, imperialism, and paternalism.

One-way mission that considers some to be superior subjects and others to be inferior objects treated with patronization and pity is not *missio Dei*. Attitudes of arrogance and unilateral actions of imposition or control do not befit God's mission. Evangelistic encounters, as well as mission service and justice initiatives with other churches, cultures, and countries, require what Bosch advocates in witness to peoples of other faiths: "an admission that we do not have all the answers and are prepared to live within the framework of penultimate knowledge, . . . a bold humility—or a humble boldness."[9] Perhaps the boldness of our individual attitudes of humility will ultimately lead to a national or church-wide "mind" or attitude of humility.

Putting Others First

James and Paul provide the Christian community with guidance for the cultivation of the attitude of humility. What does it mean in our partnerships in mission to incarnate Paul's injunction: "in humility regard others [partners] as better than yourselves" (Phil. 2:3b)? Obviously, the phrase "regard others" refers to our attitude toward others. Humility is an inner attitude toward ourselves that directly affects our attitude toward others. When we humble ourselves and assume a posture of vulnerability, we can turn to others and recognize their rightful place.

There are three basic assumptions that underlie the attitude of humility:

1. All individuals, mission partners, and groups are equally created in God's image and are "subjects" with human dignity. We all have the same intrinsic value bestowed upon us by our Creator.
2. I am/We are not better than "others." No person, race, economic class, educational status, denomination, theological position, religion, ideology, or nation can consider itself superior to "others." However, as we interact and exchange gifts, asymmetrical relationships of power come into play. Therein, assumption three is essential.
3. "Others" are better than I/we. In mission we regard our partners as better than ourselves, for they are the "others" of whom Paul speaks. This is not about intrinsic worth or earned merit. It concerns the way we treat others. They get preferential VIP treatment. It is deferring to others and giving them the best seats in the house. Missional attitudes anticipate the reign of God where the last are first, and the first are last. We emulate Christ who came "not to be served but to serve" (Mark 10:45). Mutuality in mission is always being disposed to humbly "wash one another's feet" (John 13:14). We engage in mission as strangers and guests, which means that "others" are always better than I/we.

Seeking the Interests of Others

Paul identifies the problem of selfishness or "self-interest." Earlier in the letter Paul recognizes that some minister with integrity while "others proclaim Christ out of selfish ambition" (Phil. 1:17). Later he promises to send Timothy to Philippi "so that I may be cheered by news of you. I have no one like him who will be genuinely concerned for your welfare. All of them are seeking their own interests, not those of Jesus Christ" (2:19–21). It follows naturally that if we put others first, we will seriously consider Paul's instruction: "Let each of you look not to your own interests, but to the interests of others" (2:4). It is a way of being or missional spirituality that graciously makes room in one's heart and life for others.

We unintentionally seek our own interests in mission when we "help" others in order to make us "feel good" or exercise control over others to enhance our sense of self-worth. Mission can be a kind of personal empire building or a way to assuage our guilt because we have so much. Often we assume that we know best what other nations and churches need and then impose our culture, values, and projects on them.

What would it mean for us as individuals, local congregations, denominations, and nations to empty ourselves of self-interest and selfishness and look to the interests of others? People around the world asked if the true "interests"of the United States in Iraq were the economic benefits from oil and reconstruction and the strategic control of the region or the interests of the people of Iraq. Could we be so concerned with national security that we are blinded to the interests of Arab nations and Palestinians in the Middle East? Could our refusal to heed the United Nations' guidance deafen us to the voice of the global community? Is every country's position in relation to war, nation building, and economic development based only on their own selfish interests?

A Global Perspective

How can we free ourselves from the tyranny of our own interests and learn to look intentionally and seriously to the interests and agenda of others? A place to start would be with our partner denominations and ecumenical organizations in the global church. Dialogue partners from the PC(USA), two Presbyterian denominations from Korea, and two Presbyterian denominations from Brazil met February 26 through March 16, 2000, in Korea, the United States, and Brazil to reflect on "The Reformed Faith and the Global Economy." Their concluding statement illustrates the issue of "interests":

> We urge the governments of powerful countries such as the United States to act in the international financial agencies in ways based upon the principles of democracy as is done in the domestic arena. We further urge these powerful entities to be conscious of the interest of all the people—all over the world—rather than primarily those of the most powerful, such as those who control transnational companies whose core interests are located in their own country.[10]

This joint study trip illustrates how we begin to look to the legitimate "interests of others" in our mission partnerships. Obviously, it requires a global perspective that looks beyond our own church and nation. It is a process of observing and listening to others, with special attention to excluded voices. It includes participation in the life of the other, dialogue, and critical reflection on the other's reality. The church in the West faces a crisis and is at a crossroads in worldwide mission today. Will we distance ourselves from partnership in the gospel or will we humbly assume the risks of hearing the criticism of the global church and courageously moving forward together?

Our partners worldwide are interested in living together peaceably in a multilateral international community that respects the rights and self-determination of all. Those who have suffered the downside of unfair globalization that caters to the interests of the privileged and ignores the interests of emerging nations cry out for justice and solidarity. They demand international trade agreements that are fair to all and the lifting of unnecessary sanctions that only affect the poor. Developing nations are keenly interested in sustainable development and ecological responsibility.

Christ calls each of us to examine our attitudes, to search our way of being in mission. I have learned the importance of attitudes as a mission worker in South America for over thirty years. The people I have come to respect and admire have taught me painful realities about myself, my denomination's mission activity, and my homeland. I sincerely believe that the key to mission work today is simply asking God's Spirit to progressively transform our attitudes and allowing God's grace to flow through the totality of our lives. As Paul said, "I am confident of this, that the one who began a good work among you will bring it to completion. . . . for all of you share in God's grace with me. . . . [I]t is God who is at work in you, enabling you both to will and to work for [God's] good pleasure" (Phil. 1:5, 7; 2:13).

May God's Spirit touch our inner being and grant to us a respectful attitude toward others, a compassionate re-action to the suffering of others, and a humble attitude toward ourselves as we relate to others.

PART 3   WHAT? Practices
           of Partnership

*T*he Gospels portray Jesus the missionary seeing, feeling, and acting with words and deeds. In Luke when the disciples of John the Baptist asked Jesus if he was the promised Messiah, he answered by citing his daily practices, which are signs of the presence of God's realm (Luke 7:18–23). Chapters 1–12 of the Fourth Gospel emphasize Jesus' "works" or "practices," which functioned as "signs" of his Messiahship and of God's realm of life. Jesus attends a wedding in Cana of Galilee and turns water into good wine (John 2:1–11), engages in dialogue with a Samaritan woman and with a leader of the Jews (John 3 and 4), heals a man who had been lame for thirty-eight years (5:1–15), feeds a hungry multitude (6:1–15), refuses to condemn an adulteress (8:1–11), heals a man blind from birth (John 9), raises Lazarus from the dead (John 11), is anointed by Mary with perfume (John 12), washes the disciples' feet (John 13), lays down his life for his friends (15:13), prays for others (John 17), and grills fish on the beach after his resurrection (21:4–14).

Mission begins with relationships that are characterized by the attitudes of mutual respect, compassion, and humility, but it also includes *practices.* Though we diligently seek to follow Jesus' example in our attitudes and practices, there is always room to grow and change. After all, Jesus' holistic mission is not merely activism, problem solving, or humanitarian aid. We must avoid reducing mission to benevolent actions that individual mission "practitioners" do *to* or *for* others who become "objects or recipients of the practice" and whose "larger social and historical context" is virtually ignored. The approach I will be using follows an alternative understanding of practice that Craig Dykstra proposes, "One person's action becomes practice only insofar as it is participation in the larger practice of a community and a tradition."[1] *Missio Dei* is the triune God's creative and redemptive practice in human history. The global church is called to participate in the practice of God's mission in partnership *with* God and *with* myriad others. This is why the PC(USA) has moved from "one-way" mission to "two-way" partnerships, open networks, and ever-expanding ecumenical webs of mission relationships.

Building on Dykstra's communal vision, Dorothy Bass adds, "Practices are those shared activities that address fundamental human needs and that, woven together, form a way of life."[2] Part 3 of this book reflects on mission practices that are a part of the daily life of those engaged in God's mission together in the global church. The most important dynamic in all of them is mutuality. After all, partnership begins with our mutual sharing in God's grace.

The mutuality in mission of the three persons of the Trinity is the foundation and model for all practices in mission partnerships. *Mutuality* in mission is a gift exchange, a relationship that is more horizontal than vertical and does not create dependencies or exercise domination. Mutual mission is inherently cooperative. We do things *with* one another. As we interact, we participate in mission practices together. Mutuality requires patience, openness, reciprocity, and honesty. Partners in mission create circles of mutual hospitality and seek to affirm the unique contexts, gifts, abilities, assets, and resources of all. Because of our commitment to "Mutuality and Interdependence," the PC(USA) ask the following questions together with our partners:

- Is each partner's self-reliance affirmed, with mutual giving and receiving?
- Is there space for all partners to be guided by self-determination?
- Beyond unhealthy dynamics of power and dependency, is there openness to new dynamics of mutual service and mutual renewal?[3]

Part 2 stated, *"Being" or attitudes must undergird all partner relationships and missional practices together.* Part 3 affirms, *"Being" in mission in community leads to "practicing" mission in ways that reflect the dynamics of mutuality and shared grace.*

Chapters 6 and 7 explore specific practices in the tapestry of mission partnerships. They present challenging insights on some simple mission practices, such as listening, learning, receiving, and giving. I lay out several dyads or pairs of practices in each chapter, as the titles indicate: *observing and participating* and *receiving and giving*. In mutual mission we practice both. We are both giver and receiver, both stranger and host—sometimes simultaneously. At other times we practice half of the dyad, which means someone else is practicing the other half. Then we might switch roles, which leads us to "mission-in-reverse." We retool in order to be the learner rather than the teacher or the follower rather than the leader. In mutual mission both partners are evangelized and liberated.

Chapter 8 delves back into some of the theological and biblical foundations from John's Gospel explored in chapters 1 and 2, picks up those threads again, and closes with a focus on signs of God's missional practice of *transformation*. God, and only God, transforms. The good news is that, by God's grace, persons, churches, and societies are being transformed. The chapter pulls together the final stitches in the tapestry of attitudes and practices that give God glory.

Sharing grace leads us to respond to God's call to engage in missional practices that can become God's instrument of transformation. However, we are aware that our mission practice does not always reflect our mission ideals. Our challenge today is to get our walk to match our talk, to get our practices to grow out of our desired state of being. Dykstra's affirmation engenders hope: "Practices may be deepened, enriched, extended, and to various extents be reformed and transformed."[4] Therefore, do not be conformed to old mission paradigms, but be transformed by the renewing of your missional attitudes and practices.

Chapter 6

Missional Practices:
Observing and Participating

. . . there was a wedding in Cana of Galilee, and the mother of Jesus was there. Jesus and his disciples had also been invited to the wedding.

—John 2:1–2

The Passover of the Jews was near, and Jesus went up to Jerusalem. In the temple he found people selling cattle, sheep, and doves, and the money changers seated at their tables. Making a whip of cords, he drove all of them out of the temple.

—John 2:13–15

Jesus . . . knew all people and needed no one to testify about anyone; for Jesus himself knew what was in everyone.

—John 2:24–25

*T*raditionally, we think of Jesus teaching, preaching, and healing. What were his other missional practices? How do the "signs" in John help us understand these practices?

In the Fourth Gospel Jesus participated in weddings and in funerals. Jesus practiced his mission in the obscure rural peripheries of Galilee and in the powerful center of Jerusalem. How much time did he spend observing people at the wedding in Cana? How many glasses of wine did Jesus enjoy around tables while celebrating life with others? How long did he sit in silent observation weaving a whip of cords before his angry clash with the commerce of religion in the temple in Jerusalem? What were Jesus' thoughts when he observed and fully comprehended the fragile and sinful condition of humankind? The evangelist records important words and discourses of Jesus, but how many hours did Jesus spend on the road, around the table, by the seaside, and in the temple listening to the thoughts and questions of others? Our compassionate Lord, who shared the suffering of the sick, the dying, and persons on the Galilean margins, suffered opposition and finally completed his mission by suffering the pain of betrayal, denial, and abandonment on the cross. The Master who often declared, "My hour has not yet come," waited and at last prayed, "The hour has come" (John 17:1). Jesus modeled many missional practices.

Observing and Participating

In the past missionaries were pioneers, leaders, translators, and teachers. The positive result of frontier missionary work is that the "mustard seed" of the gospel has grown into a worldwide church. As we enter the twenty-first century, partners in mission are cultivating new skills and practices for new challenges. First and foremost beyond any other tasks or activity, as *active subjects* engaged in mission partnerships today, we are *both* observer and participant.

The mission of the church only becomes a possibility when we are able to observe what God is doing in the world and then participate in that activity, the practice of *missio Dei*. It is not easy for us to see beyond our own activities and lifestyle in order to discern God's caring project of fullness of life for all. In spite of the signs of disgrace that abound in the world and in the church, we still believe that God is passionately and pastorally involved in human history. Jesus came announcing that God's realm or reign of peace, love, joy, and justice is "already" present on earth, but "not yet" consummated and complete. Only the triune God can finish God's mission and fully establish God's realm. God graciously invites us to join in the divine activities of redemption, healing, and transformation. Our mission does not usher in utopia or God's realm, but we hope to erect signs of it. We participate in mission practices with a creative tension between the "already" and the "not yet," between the empirical reality of this world and the prophetic imagination of "a new heaven and a new earth" (Rev. 21:1), oscillating between joy and agony.

Participant observation and its twin, observant participation, are the intentional practices by which outsiders seek to follow the model of the Word who "became flesh and lived among us" eating, drinking, sleeping, laughing, weeping, talking, listening, touching, playing, praying, suffering, dying, and rising. Though missionaries are always outsiders, incarnational mission requires participation with and awareness of the life of the other. Sensitive observation leads to perception, discernment, and learning. Out of this grows deeper participation that enables understanding and identification and hopes for some level of incorporation. Observing and participating in authentic ways show the measure of our respect for others and ourselves as God's children. Moreover, outside participants admit their need for hospitality and partner relationships and accept their state of indebtedness and vulnerability. Indeed, mission tasks rest on these fundamental bases.

The first step to observing and participating is humbly relinquishing control and initiative and being quiet and attentive. To observe is to see beyond our own concerns, opinions, agendas, customs, and interpretations. Like birdwatchers, we stop, look, and listen. We can learn much about culture and faith by observing children. By observing verbal and body language, we begin to penetrate the layers of culture as in peeling an onion. Observers participate by taking advantage of opportunities and open doors. They accept invitations to take part in the activities of others. There are many different ways and levels of participation. We must know when to observe and when to participate, and we must not forget to be observant when we are participating.

Missionaries who come to the United States are able to perceptively assume the posture of "flies on a wall" who carefully observe everything and everyone before speaking. They seek to read the context and the signs of the times. An example of the cutting-edge insights obtained through such observing and participating can be seen in the book *A Strange Accent: the Reflections of a Missionary to the United States.* It contains penetrating sermons preached by Thomas John, a professor and pastor in the Church of South India, while he was a Mission Partner in Residence for the PC(USA). This cross-cultural practice of observing is not natural for us from the United States. Because of our dominant culture, we often tend to be more like "bulls in a china shop." At times we speak out as though we are experts on another country that we have briefly visited when in reality we spent very little time truly and attentively observing.

The cultivation of this missional practice entails intentional observation of individuals, families, leaders, followers, the excluded, congregations, denominations, societies, structures, local and global events, rituals, and relationships. Participant observers seek to be aware of cultural, social, economic, political, and religious elements of the reality of the other. We graciously and as inconspicuously as possible participate in daily life, table fellowship, commercial exchanges, church services and meetings, as well as local events at the invitation of our hosts.

Persons engaged in missional practices in contexts or cultures different from their own will always be strangers and outsiders. Our attitudes and relationships to our mission partners who are hosts and insiders determine our potential contribution and our personal benefit. As Anthony Gittins says,

> The stranger can aspire to being a participating outsider, so long as the stranger remains an outsider and yet participates. To remain an outsider means not to assume too much, not to make inappropriate demands, to remain socially marginal (servant), to be disinterested (not clinging to status). To participate means to discover one's place on the agenda, to contribute to the felt needs of the community, to be a servant, yet to be able to challenge and support, to be spiritually and culturally life-transmitting and life-propagating. These are challenges for every missionary stranger.[1]

Listening and Speaking

We observe by "seeing" and also by listening or "hearing." In mission we must listen to God and to Christ's story as revealed in Scripture. We thus go to other countries, churches, and cultures as listeners and learners like "Mary, who sat at the Lord's feet and listened to what he was saying" (Luke 10:39). We listen, ask and answer questions, and speak when appropriate. Honest listening, open dialogue, and authentic respect make possible mutual partnerships.

Both reverent silence and creative words are powerful. After all, God spoke and the world was created. God heard the cries of the oppressed (Gen. 16:11; Exod. 3:7). Jesus Christ, who came as the incarnate Word of God, was also a radical listener. The Emmaus story in Luke's Gospel (24:13–35) illustrates Jesus' ability and disposition to listen. The two disciples on the road were depressed, disappointed, and disillusioned because of the death of Jesus. They refused to listen to the report of the women who talked about resurrection. Jesus "came near and went with them" and initiated a conversation with a question: " 'What are you discussing with each other while you walk along?' " (v. 17). They immediately identify him as an outsider and stranger and ask, " 'Are you the only stranger in Jerusalem who does not know the things that have taken place there in these days?' " (v. 18). If you were Jesus, how would you have answered that question? Was there anyone more on the "inside" of the crucifixion than Jesus? Could anyone tell the story more accurately than Jesus? What was his answer? Another question: " 'What things?' " (v. 19). Then the crucified and risen Lord patiently and attentively listened to their story before he shared a greater story and later accepted their invitation to table fellowship.

Through the practice or discipline of listening, we not only seek to discern God's will and signs of God's transforming activity, but we also get to know others and hear their stories and life experiences. By responding appropriately, the miracles of dialogue and reciprocity are possible.

We must resist the temptation of our goal-driven, multitask-oriented Western culture to be in constant activity. Perhaps the "one thing" that is most needful today in mission is to refrain from obsessive doing and speaking and concentrate on authentic listening to the nonverbal and verbal messages of the people with whom we live and work. We must develop the ability to hold silence and not talk. Listening requires humility, vulnerability, availability, receptivity, and patience. Even when we provide opportunities for visiting partners to speak in our churches, mission conferences, denominational offices, and presbytery meetings, we must have patience to be interrupted and to listen to English with accents and translations. True listening hears the pain, frustration, fear, hostility, and hopelessness lurking behind words. Rather than coming to a mission task with control and answers, we come to listen and be in dialogue.

Presbyterians involved in mission together practice the policy principle of "Open Dialogue and Transparency." It leads us to ask the following questions in our partner relationships:

- Is there local initiative in mission discernment and mission activity?
- Does God's Word shape us to lovingly confront one another's failings and prophetically challenge the world's systems of power and domination?
- Is there transparency with all partners about what is being done in mission, even if there is disagreement?[2]

Genuine dialogue is essential in mission partnerships. Every person and every partner has a right to speak and to be heard. However, it is time for those who have traditionally assumed the role of speakers to learn how to listen. After all, there is "a time to keep silence, and a time to speak" (Eccl. 3:7b). Likewise, it is time for those who have rarely had the opportunity to speak, or whose voice has not been heard, to step forth and speak. In other words, mission today calls for surprising role reversals.

Sharing Sufferings and Suffering

If we seriously observe, listen, and participate in the lives of our partners around the world and of people in our cities who are different from us, we will see and feel their struggles, pain, and suffering. People all around us suffer from hunger, disease, poverty, injustice, ignorance, loneliness, and violence. Unfortunately, members of our global partner churches who are in the United

States suffer unintentional discrimination and humiliation every day simply because they are poorer and have darker skin. It is hypocritical to share in the struggles of our sisters and brothers far away and to ignore the suffering of those nearby. The missional practice of suffering and sharing in sufferings is in many respects "the most profound and difficult of all manifestations of partnership."[3]

The report from the section on "Participating in Suffering and Struggle" of the World Council of Churches' conference on mission and evangelism held in San Antonio, Texas, in 1989 begins with this powerful statement: "Participation in suffering and struggle is at the heart of God's mission and God's will for the world. It is central for our understanding of the incarnation, the most glorious example of participation in suffering and struggle. The church is sent in the way of Christ bearing the marks of the cross in the power of the Holy Spirit (cf. John 20:19–23)." The report concludes with a compelling invitation: "Churches are invited to recognize the wind and fire of the presence of the Spirit wherever the suffering cry out, and by participating in their struggles in the way of Christ, to become part of the good news for them, bearing witness that God wills for them and for all people, life in fullness."[4]

Participating in God's mission is rewarding, but it is also a dangerous practice. Not only do we share in the sufferings of others, but we also may be called to suffer. Mission is risk-taking, self-denial, and sacrifice. Mission challenges the status quo and embodies an alternative consciousness. It is often prophetically subversive, moving us out of secure comfort zones and sending us to the edges and margins of life. After all, the Greek word for witness is *martyria.* Beginning with Stephen (Acts 7), the history of the church is bathed with the blood of martyrs. When we contemplate the call/conversion of Saul/Paul, we must not forget God's solemn words, "'I myself will show him how much he must *suffer* for the sake of my name'" (Acts 9:16).

Paul exhorts the Romans to "weep with those who weep" (12:15). In his first letter to the church in Corinth, he writes, "If one member suffers, all suffer together with it" (12:26). In 2 Corinthians he tells them that they share in the sufferings of Christ because "you patiently endure the same sufferings that we are also suffering . . . you share in our sufferings, so also you share in our consolation" (1:6, 7). Likewise, to the Philippians Paul expresses his desire to "know Christ and the power of his resurrection and the sharing of his sufferings by becoming like him in his death" (3:10). However daunting and countercultural it may seem, our partnership with God and with others can lead to our suffering and to sharing the sufferings of others.

We share in the sufferings of others by being present, by participating in their struggles, by feeling their pain, by reacting with compassion, and by joining them in solidarity as advocates. We who tend to think we don't have sufferings of our own need the vulnerability, openness, and honesty to name our hurts and to invite our partners to join our struggles, to feel our pain, and to be present with us in our time of need. Partners share the sufferings of one another and mutually comfort and encourage one another. As Walter Brueggemann says, "Suffering made audible and visible produces hope, articulated grief is the gate of newness, and the history of Jesus is the history of entering into the pain and giving it voice."[5] Partners enter into the labor and labor pains of one another.

Sharing Joys and Celebrating

I taught a course on mission in partnership to around thirty students from what seemed like thirty denominations at the Evangelical Theological Faculty in Concepción, Chile. In one class I presented the missional practices contained in this chapter. Then the students divided into groups and reflected on case studies. When they came back to share, I asked them for corrections, applications, and suggestions in relation to the practices we had studied. One student perceptively asked, "What about the second half of 1 Corinthians 12:26: 'If one member is honored, all rejoice together with it'? We also share joys and celebrate with others. Shouldn't you add that as a mission practice?" Of course! Then we remembered the other half of Romans 12:15: "Rejoice with those who rejoice." Latin Americans have taught me not only what it means to be in solidarity with those who suffer, but also the importance and joy of celebrating life together. It seems that those who most profoundly experience suffering are the ones who most intensely celebrate joy. *Fiestas* are at the heart of Latin culture. Birthdays, wedding anniversaries, baptisms, church anniversaries, inaugurations, and other commemorative occasions all provide opportunities to enjoy and celebrate life with music, laughter, and food. Musical instruments, lively Latin American rhythms, and corporal interpretations express their zest and passion for life. Worship services are joyful celebrations. Palm Sunday processionals and "hosannas" in Roman Catholic churches capture the festive movement of Jesus and his followers.

When we were gathering resources from our partners south of the border for the Year with Latin Americans initiative, we selected as the title for our publication *A Celebration of Life: Gifts from Latin Americans*. The liturgical and reflective gifts that our partners offered were an invitation to "Join the celebration *and* the struggle!" Sometimes we need to escape from our hectic lives in order to stop and smell the fragrance of the roses, to share the simple joys of living in God's world and in human community. As I write, I am drinking tea out of a colorful mug that one of those Chilean students washed and spontaneously offered to me as the class joyfully and with simplicity celebrated our week together on the last evening. He unselfishly gave to me the mug that he was using to drink tea on that very cold night. It reminds me of the joy the students shared with me and one another in and out of the classroom during that time.

Waiting and Praying

In Biblical times the Israelites participated in their great festivals with joy and vigor, celebrating God's past acts of deliverance. They were encouraged and filled with hope by the prophets' future visions of restored community and creation (Isa. 65:20–25). However, when the Hebrew prophets shared the sufferings of God's people, they often asked, "How long, Lord?" They waited on the salvation of God, but not passively or with resignation. In his final instructions Jesus told the disciples "not to leave Jerusalem, but to wait there for the promise of the Father" (Acts 1:4). They didn't understand waiting as a missional practice and were anxious for Roman oppression to end, so they asked him, " 'Lord, is this the time when you will restore the kingdom to Israel?' " (Acts 1:6). Jesus reminded them that God is sovereign and determines the times and ways of God's mission. After Jesus' ascension, the first action of the commissioned men and women was to wait and pray (Acts 1:14).

Chapter 1 of Acts portrays the importance of waiting and praying as a preface and preparation to Pentecost and the birth of the church (Acts 2). In mission we are completely dependent on God's action and timing. The theme of prayer echoes throughout Acts as the church prays for boldness and as the Spirit opens and closes doors for the apostles, deacons, Paul, and his partners in mission who seek God's will and wait for God's guidance.

It was while "they were worshiping the Lord" that the Holy Spirit said to the church at Antioch, " 'Set apart for me Barnabas and Saul for the work to which I have called them' " (Acts 13:2). Indeed, the church is a worshiping community, for the ultimate goal of all our mission is giving glory to God (John 17:4). Whenever the worshiping community gathers, we examine attitudes, recognize weaknesses, and ask God to transform us and send us in mission. We listen to God's Word and open ourselves to allow God's Spirit to act in and through us. We pray for our local congregations in mission; for mission in our neighborhoods, cities, and nation; for the world; for the global

church in mission; for our mission partners; and for suffering people everywhere whose cries we have observed and heard.

Prayer proceeds and accompanies all other mission practices. *Prayer is*
mission. Missional prayer reaches out beyond our walls and lives to embrace
the entire world. Waiting in hope is a practice essential in all mission. Partners wait on each other, pray for one another, and worship God together. The
PC(USA) *Manual for International Mission Partnerships* suggests easy and
natural ways to maintain partnerships: pray together, even when apart; worship together, even when apart; study together, even when apart; visit one
another; and jointly plan activities. Worship is greatly enriched when it is multicultural. To say the Lord's Prayer in many languages is a sign of the plenitude of God's creative realm, a foretaste of the eschatological banquet.

Human participation in God's mission begins and continues with the
prayer that propels us into mission with hope: "Your kingdom come, your
will be done." The Brazilian Rubem Alves has a wondrous meditation on the
phrase in the Lord's Prayer "Your kingdom come" entitled "Appetizers of
the Future."[6] The poem tells the story of a father waiting late on a rainy night
for the arrival of his son. He strains to hear the familiar sound of his car. The
dark neighborhood indicates serene sleep where no one is far away. The poet
explains, "It is not the distance that hurts. What hurts is the desire. I don't
miss people I have never seen or places I have never loved. . . . It is necessary to love first. Only then is distance filled with pain." The poet remembers
the tears of a lover, who in each hug of greeting already anticipated the hug
of departure. He reflects back on his son, "Indeed, in the waiting, is hidden,
the joy of presence and the fear of solitude. Therein the silent prayer 'Please,
come.'"

The poet ponders the beauty and vicissitudes of the world, which are like
pieces of a puzzle. "Fragments of a past. . . . Fragments of a future. . . . Will
there be something different? We harvest the past, memories of joys. Appetizers, messengers of lost times worth seeking. . . ."

"Appetizers? From the future perfumes come to us, whispers of voices, and
the wind serves us fragments, sacraments. . . . In each piece of bread, in each
swallow of wine."

Appetizers in rivers, organ music, streams in the desert, sounds of oceans,
smells of food, of animals, of people, tastes of fruits and skin, tenderness of
sun, rain, wind, folks.

Until finally, "The entire 'uni/verse' sighs, waits, prays, like a mother:
'Please, come.'"

"And your verse? Sing it too: it will be your prayer. It's easy. Just say the
names of things, images that appear: Your kingdom come."

Dreams: names of children expected in the middle of the night. . . .
The man, hoe in hand, dreams about land. . . .
Woman, child at breast, dreams about a home. . . .
Child, with nothing in hand, plays with the dream. . . .
Those who die of hunger dream about bread,
those who die in war dream about laps,
hands without weapons,
lullabies from the mouth of Pietás,
beautiful mothers,
tender mothers, eternal. . . .
Fragments of the body of God,
dilacerated:
our food.
We eat,
we drink. . . .

Finally, at the end of the poem, the poet envisions fish swimming upstream to reproduce and concludes with this verse:

We too: love a time that has not yet arrived.
It grows within us.
And our gestures become dances/magical struggles. . . .
Of the future, songs that for a long time. . . .
Hope: we hear them. . . .
Faith: we dance them. . . .
"Your kingdom come."

Chapter 7

Missional Practices: Receiving and Giving

[God] gives the Spirit without measure.

—*John 3:34*

I give them eternal life, and they will never perish.

—*John 10:29*

Peace I leave with you; my peace I give to you.

—*John 14:27*

I have given them your word.

—*John 17:14*

Receive the Holy Spirit.

—*John 20:22*

An invitation to deliver purchases to the home of "the aristocrat of Black Stamps" was the "first life line" for young Maya Angelou. She was served cookies and lemonade and received her first loaned book. In her attempt to recover the "enchantment I so easily found in those gifts," Maya says, "the essence escapes but its aura remains. To be allowed, no, invited, into the private lives of strangers, and to share their joys and fears, was a chance to exchange the Southern bitter wormwood for a cup of mead with Beowulf or a hot cup of tea and milk with Oliver Twist. . . . I was liked, and what a difference it made. I was respected . . . for just being Marguerite Johnson."[1]

Receiving and Giving

The triune God is self-giving and other-receiving, never enclosed or turned inward. God's love overflows and pours itself forth as life. Love never stops giving and receiving. The love and life God gives to the world are altogether gift. God is giver, gift, and gift exchanger. The language of Father, Son, and Spirit in the Fourth Gospel shows that God is profoundly relational. The mutuality inherent in the Trinity is the source and model for all practices in mission partnerships. Mutuality in mission is a *gift exchange,* an ongoing two-way relationship of giving and receiving. Partnership built on gift exchange is a form of radical relatedness to God and to others. Partnership is a mutual sharing of grace in spiritual gifts, material resources, and suffering.

"For God so loved the world that [God] gave [God's] only Son, so that everyone who believes in [Jesus] may not perish but may have eternal life" (John 3:16). Jesus came into the world as a sheer gift of God's abundant grace. The self-gift of the Shepherd of love was most evident at the last supper and on the cross. God loves. God gives. God sends. God offers "gifts," but never forces people to accept them. God invites a response, an act of reception. Our response is only possible because God first gives and loves. We love because God first loves us. We give because God, the giver of "every perfect gift" (James 1:17), first gives.

How do we respond? What can we give to God in return? We receive. We believe. "To all who received him, who believed in his name, [God] gave power to become children of God. . . . From [God's] fullness we have all received, grace upon grace" (John 1:12). As Michael Downey explains in *Altogether Gift,* "Our first response to gift is not to respond, but to receive. And then, without burden of cost or interest, to live freely with, in, and from the gift."[2] In response to God's gift of love, we give our thanksgiving, praise, and adoration. We present our lives as living sacrifices. God receives. Anthony Gittens explains our obligation and God's:

> If we have a relationship with God, we have an obligation to give, to receive, and to return. If God has a relationship with us, God has a relationship to give and receive and return. . . . God *must* give because God is self-giving. God *must* receive because God is gracious. God *must* return because God is in relationship. But we too *must* give because all we have belongs to God. We *must* receive in order to live. And we *must* return because we need relationship (italics in the original).[3]

We enter into a mutual relationship of receiving and giving with God and God's world. We receive grace, live in grace, and share grace with all. As children and heirs, we participate in God's life and mission, as recipients of both gift and task. Mission is our Spirit-enabled response of self-giving and other-receiving. Learning to do this has not been easy for North American Christians. The church's historical role has been that of benevolent patron and dispenser of charity. One-way mission is basically gift giving by the rich and powerful to the less fortunate. We are professional givers who decide what is needed, what to give, and how to use the gift. Through generous and sacrificial giving of money and lives to the church's mission work, myriad churches, schools, and hospitals have been established on every continent. These institutions now are often administered by national Christians of autonomous denominations.

Does unidirectional gift giving cause problems? What are the relational consequences of mission out of affluence? Gift giving can foster the illusion of superiority because it gives power or control to the giver. Gifts usually help but can also humiliate the recipient, who becomes indebted to the giver. This indebtedness creates the possibility of reciprocity and an ongoing relationship. However, when there is no reciprocity, unidirectional giving spawns dependency and resentment.

Unfortunately, the mission work, lifestyle, and abundant resources of affluent churches symbolize the unequal distribution of global wealth and the domination of those who have much. Resistance to global inequality often finds expression by mission partners who have fewer financial resources. Such resistance shows itself in many forms, such as mistrust, envy, competition, begging (requests), and reverse exploitation (taking advantage). Partners make continual requests for large grants and expect to receive them. Individuals form relationships with congregations who constantly supply their needs and wants; these relationships, in turn, create an unhealthy dependency that can breed envy or resentment. In other words, our well-intentioned generosity and excessive gifts can suffocate our partner's dignity and initiative.

In *gift exchange* all partners practice *both* receiving and giving in a spirit of mutual respect that results in mutual enrichment. How do we move beyond paternalistic gift giving to gift exchange that promotes relationships of interdependence, reciprocity, and mutuality? First of all, we must empty ourselves of self-sufficiency, autonomy, and independence so that we can *learn how to graciously receive* gifts from our partners. This entails a spirit of openness, vulnerability, and need of the other. A part of one's self is shared in a true gift exchange, so we open ourselves to receive the other. We then recognize and value the dignity and gifts of others. We acknowledge our indebtedness to the other and wait for the appropriate opportunity to reciprocate. There is no hurry. It is good to be in the other's debt for a while.

What might we receive from our partners? How might a partner minister to us? Jon Sobrino presents a model in which "loving co-responsibility is achieved through the mutual giving and receiving of churches to and from one another. This giving and receiving should be extended to diverse areas of the life of the church—liturgical, pastoral, and theological—but based on something yet more fundamental: giving and receiving in the practice of faith."[4] He continues, "The poor offer their own poverty as a questioning of the way that being human is understood and as another possible way to be human. When the poor live their poverty with spirit, with gospel values, with courage in persecution, with hope in their struggles, with the kind of love that can sustain martyrdom, what they are offering is simply their faith."[5]

Visiting groups and mission workers testify to gifts they have received: hand-crafted treasures; incarnations of humility, simplicity, joy, and solidarity; demonstrations of relational values; new eyes for reading Scripture and world; renewed meaning and direction in life; an awareness of their need for continued conversion; and questioning of values in their culture.

Secondly, we must *learn how, what, and when to give* with humility and compassion in a way that honors, dignifies, and respects others. This requires extraordinary sensitivity to cultural differences and issues. It is important to get to know one another and to pray with and for one another before offering financial assistance. A rule of thumb in presbytery partnerships is to wait a couple of years before discussing money matters. It is always best for projects to be initiated and owned by those who will sustain them over time. Only insiders know their own needs and priorities. Often partners seek outside resources as "seed" money to initiate programs or "matching" grants to complete projects. The PC(USA) encourages sustainable development. Discerning donors are careful not to overwhelm partners with gifts that will be difficult to manage, sustain, and fit into the cultural context. Untimely financial gifts or a one-way flow of money can cause great problems. Sometimes the most precious missional gifts are not material or financial ones but gifts of recognition and personal presence received in the practices of observing, participating, listening, sharing sufferings and joys, waiting, praying, and worshiping together.

All partners are involved in ongoing giving, receiving, and reciprocating. All have the right and obligation to give and the right and obligation to receive. In order to give and receive with discerning wisdom, partners in mission continually ask, What are the unique gifts, abilities, assets, opportunities, and resources of all partners? Partners develop a long-term compassionate bond of mutual indebtedness, mutual accountability, and gift exchange. Putting relationships first makes inequalities less problematic, since there is no way to measure the value of a relationship's intangible and interpersonal gifts. While mission entails sharing people and resources, mutuality and reciprocity are the measure of genuine nonhierarchical, nonpatronizing, mutually deferring partnerships of shared grace and faith.

Learning and Teaching

One gift that we receive from others is knowledge; thus learning from others is one way to receive. We learn much unintentionally through informal exchanges and models, as well as from intentional instruction. Like receiving, learning is a cutting-edge challenge for PC(USA) mission participants. We are much more accustomed to giving and teaching.

Christ calls Christians to "learn from me" (Matt. 11:29) and to make and be disciples (Matt. 28:19) or life-long learners. One of the signs of God's reign is a reversal of roles. Some who have been last are now leading the global Church-in-mission, and some who have been first are now last (Luke 13:29–30) and are learning to follow, receive, listen, and learn.

In order to learn from others, we leave our comfort zone and go to where people are. We go to the streets, to public places, and to the turf of the other. We visit people in their homes, churches, and places of work. We approach partners with an intentional openness to see, listen, and learn. A humble attitude produces a teachable spirit. As we observe the values, attitudes, practices, and behavior of others, we learn much about prayer, ethics, and evangelism. In worship and dialogue with Christians whose background is different from ours, we gain a better knowledge of God, the world, love, and truth. From those who have suffered injustices and violence, we discover the social implications of the gospel. The body language of people can teach us what it means to be full of joy and peace. As we spend time asking questions and listening to the stories, experiences, interpretations, explanations, and opinions of sisters and brothers from around the world, we learn about church, ecology, family, and social responsibility. When we listen attentively to second languages with accents or hear translations of sermons from cultural and theological perspectives that are unlike ours, our faith matures.

God's mission sends the Holy Spirit to gift and teach human mission agents (John 14:26). Paul reminds the Corinthian Christians that "God chose what is foolish in the world to shame the wise; God chose what is weak in the world to shame the strong; God chose what is low and despised in the world . . . so that no one might boast in the presence of God" (1 Cor. 1:27–29). The apostle practiced mission out of weakness and in dependence on the Spirit "so that your faith might rest not on human wisdom but on the power of God" (1 Cor. 2:5). Roles are often reversed in God's reign of reciprocity.

Every child of God has something to give us and something to teach us. Jesus showed that children, women, those who suffer, the marginalized, people of oral traditions, and persons of other religions and cultures can teach us more than we expect. Michael Downey speaks profoundly about what the strong can learn from the weak. Downey says, "The handicapped, the wounded and the weak, the last, the littlest, and the least often remind the clever and the robust that the chief characteristic of the human is to be open to relationship with others, to be constantly open to the Gift/ing which binds us together in a communion of Love."[6]

In all of the dyads of missional practices discussed in chapters 6 and 7, we assume both roles. While the learning curve of disciples in the northern hemisphere is the discipline of receiving and learning from disciples in the southern hemisphere, all of us continue to teach. Those of us with the gift of teaching can't stay out of the classroom too long, though the world is our classroom. At times we teach each other the painful lessons we have learned about our own biases, prejudices, and insensitivities. As one African American said, "I'm tired of teaching white folk how to be culturally sensitive. They need to teach themselves." Diverse opportunities abound for short- and long-term teaching in mission situations at home and abroad.

Building Community and Empowering Builders

Much of the church's mission work has involved building. The notable legacy of missionary brick and mortar can be seen in churches, schools, and hospitals around the globe. Because of our cultural propensity for measurable tasks and concrete projects, there is nothing that groups from local congregations would rather do than a construction project. As a result, many less fortunate people now are proud homeowners. Yet what else might we build? What if building partnerships, relationships, and community became our priority? What if building bridges between communities, religions, peoples, cultures, and nations challenged us to move beyond our isolation and individualism? What if empowering builders took precedence over laying bricks? Indeed, what if? A world of endless possibilities unfolds!

When Jesus said, " 'I will build my church' " (Matt. 16:18), he was not talking about a building or earthly kingdom. Jesus envisioned a global community of disciples. God's missionary par excellence wrote no books and constructed no buildings, but he built up and empowered a community. Jesus said to Peter and the disciples, " 'I will give you the keys of the kingdom of heaven' " (Matt. 16:19). Jesus built his followers into a community, practiced his mission with that community, and entrusted it with missionary authority and pastoral responsibility.

God gave human beings diverse spiritual gifts "to equip the saints for the work of ministry, for building up the body of Christ" (Eph. 4:12). Paul makes it clear that mission is a partnership in which "the one who plants and the one who waters have a common purpose," but only God gives the growth (1 Cor. 3:7, 8). Paul continues, "For we are God's servants, working together; you are . . . God's building" (v. 9) and then compares himself to "a skilled master builder" who lays a foundation (Jesus Christ) on which someone else is building (v. 10). The apostle goes on to advise, "Each builder must choose with care how to build" on the foundation (v. 10b).

How do we help build each other up in the body of Christ into a global community of solidarity? Whether we empower builders, build community, or construct edifices, we do it with respect, compassion, and humility through hands that heal, smiles that welcome, hugs that forgive, words that encourage, and hope that builds peace in spite of war. We do this because we are baptized into a community. We become and mature as disciples in the context of community. The more diverse, extended, and welcoming the community is, the more complete we become as persons, society, and creation.

What does it mean to empower others to build? Every disciple and every Christian community and denomination has the right, the privilege, and the responsibility to build up and propagate the body of Christ in their place. Each part of the universal church invests spiritual, human, and material resources according to their gifts, context, and priorities. We empower others to build by trusting them with the "keys," by respecting their cultural way of being and doing church. Mission in partnership is not building church or community *for* others, or simply *with* others, but working together in the church *of* others. We learn to give up control, share responsibility, and live the good news of Jesus Christ in community with others who build.

By building community and empowering builders we participate in building up the faith of the universal church. We affirm and practice the catholicity of Christ's church. The building of community is related to the primacy of relationship in gift exchange. Perhaps the quality of our building practice is commensurate to the depth of our relationships. Missional practices are communal. We build and are built up through mutual receiving and giving and mutual learning and teaching. We overcome our selfishness and parochialism as we "build up each other" (1 Thess. 5:11) into a worldwide community of believers in Jesus Christ.

Receiving Witnesses and Witnessing

The global faith community is a witness to and a sign of the presence and transforming power of the reign of God in the world. Jesus Christ inaugurated on earth God's peaceful realm of joy and fullness of life for all. The "signs" recorded in the Fourth Gospel demonstrate God's saving intentions for humankind and creation. The disciples were eyewitnesses to the life, ministry, death, resurrection, and ascension of Christ. They were sent into the world in the manner of John the baptizer who "came as a witness to testify to the light, so that all might believe through him" (John 1:7). Like the Samaritan woman at the well (John 4:29, 39), they gave testimony of their encounter and experience with Jesus and invited others to "come and see." Before his departure, Jesus promised to send the Spirit of truth who "will testify on my behalf. You also are to testify because you have been with me from the beginning" (John 15:26–27). The book of Acts narrates the fulfillment of the promise: "You will receive power when the Holy Spirit has come upon you; and you will be my witnesses in Jerusalem, in all Judea and Samaria, and to the ends of the earth" (1:8).

God loves the world. God gives life. God sent the Savior to the world. We receive God's gracious gift. We respond. We give witness. Others give witness. We receive their witness. Witness is a response that invites a response of others. Witness is invitational. Witness invites and helps people make a decision in response to God's grace. It is intrinsic to the joyful message of the gospel that it can be received, responded to, experienced, witnessed, observed, demonstrated, passed on, shared, lived, and authenticated. Therefore, all missional attitudes and practices witness to the gospel message and realm of God. For this reason Darrell Guder understands mission as witness that includes "the witness as person (the *being* of witness), the witness as action (the *doing* of witness), and witness as communication (the *saying* of witness)" (italics in the original).[7]

The early Christian communities often paid a dear price as "witnesses" (from the root *martyr*) to Jesus and the gospel message. For two millennia followers of Christ have continued to bear testimony to God's redemptive actions in Christ. Today the "center of gravity" of the church has shifted to the southern hemisphere. We receive the witness of the global church. Churches in China, Cuba, and Eastern Europe witness to God's faithfulness during repressive regimes. Contagious church growth in Africa demonstrates Spirit-powered indigenous evangelism. Korean believers testify to the importance of daily prayer vigils and mission vision. Pentecostals in Latin America witness to the joy of the Lord, while the voice and blood of others is a witness to truth and justice. We humbly receive the vibrant witness of our sisters and brothers.

While the life of a community is its primary witness, Christian worship also is a witness to the faithfulness and gratuity of God's realm. When God's children gather around the table without distinctions to receive bread and wine, we anticipate the fullness of God's realm of plenitude and equality. When we visit partner churches in other places and participate in worship, we receive the gift of their witness to God's healing love and providence. When we open ourselves and extend hospitality to partners who come to visit us, we receive a living demonstration of the power of the gospel. We can learn much more than we ever imagined from these witnesses. Our hospitality could lead to our own continuing evangelization, conversion, and transformation.

Does the PC(USA) still practice verbal witness or evangelism? Yes! Our baptism calls us to share the good news by our attitudes and practices, by our lives and words. Worldwide Ministries Division has an Office of International Evangelism to which is assigned not only budget resources but a fourth of our mission personnel. Because of past and present disrespectful techniques and our advocacy of religious tolerance, we seek holistic approaches and appropriate ways to witness to God's grace at home and around the world. We recognize the importance of training and equipping indigenous leaders in evangelism since they are much more effective than outsiders. Often the bold and spontaneous witness of our partners in other lands liberates us from our inhibitions about sharing the gospel message with words. While our lives speak louder than our words, we also need to learn to verbalize spontaneously our faith and hope.

Being Healed and Healing

God's mission heals broken humanity and creation. All healing is rooted in the triune relational God who desires right relationships between Creator and creatures, among human creatures, and between creatures and creation. The Creator makes no separation between material and spiritual and intends wholeness or *shalom* for all. God creates, redeems, heals, and "abides" in the whole person and the whole universe. The incarnation of Jesus was the embodiment of God's love. Jesus touched and anointed the sick. The evangelist summarizes: "Jesus went about all the cities and villages, teaching in their synagogues, and proclaiming the good news of the kingdom, and curing every disease and every sickness" (Matt. 9:35). Each healing was a "sign" or demonstration of God's gratuitous love for humanity and society.

Experiences of healing and the search for wholeness are of growing importance in the global church today. The world is burdened with sickness and disease. In Africa AIDS is destroying an entire generation. Open wounds are everywhere. Human existence is fragmented. Holistic mission articulates a total gospel that initiates a healing process of the total person and seeks the integrity of society and creation. Healing includes nutrition, prevention, medications, health facilities, community development, and home care. We seek to empower health care systems for sustainability. We join people on every continent in their struggle with hunger, poverty, disaster, and disease—against malaria, tuberculosis, and HIV/AIDS.

Shared grace heals bodies and relationships and cultivates healing communities. We are called to be, in Henri Nouwen's words, "wounded healers," not fixers. Anthony Gittens presents a cross-cultural perspective on healing and wholeness and encourages us to journey beyond our safe havens to the dangerous edge of the pains we fear and to build communities of trust and mutuality with others. "How can there be a collaborative community of healers unless there is real mutuality that is unafraid of questions, and not embarrassed to be seen in compassionate as well as in rational roles, prepared to be ministered to as well as to seize the opportunity to minister?"[8] The other partner, a stranger, can "uniquely fulfill a crucial function: they may open our eyes, illuminate our horizons, and offer new and unexpected perspectives."[9]

The practice of healing persons, relationships, families, communities, nations, and creation involves a gamut of healing practices: the practice of forgiveness, justice, reconciliation, and peace. All of us are wounded. Our weakness and fragility are part of our condition as human persons, of having a body, of being embodied. In a spirit of vulnerability, openness, and receptivity, we admit that we need to be touched, healed, and forgiven by others.

In our mission work we have caused many wounds in lives, churches, and cultures around the world. People harbor many dangerous memories of missionary insensitivity and imposition. We have caused divisions and resentments to fester. We have transported the racism that is part of our cultural legacy. The practice of healing begins with the prayers, "Lord, be merciful to me a sinner," and "Forgive us our sins, as we forgive those who have sinned against us."

"Mission in Reverse"

Ultimately, we are back to the traditional missional practices of Jesus: teaching, proclaiming, and healing. Presbyterians major in educating, evangelizing, and healing. Is there anything new under the sun? Yes, this book emphasizes *a new way* of doing mission with mutuality, respect, and humility. Partnerships are based on sharing, on reciprocal receiving and giving. "Mission in reverse" is discovering new roles on the other side of the dyad and new images for mission work. We have examined old and new practices with new lens "from below."

The practices in this chapter, all under the rubric of giving and receiving, are reflected in the title of the new PC(USA) vision statement: *Gathering for God's Future: Witness, Discipleship, Community.* However, these old practices must be done in new ways if we are going to rise to the four crucial challenges for worldwide ministry in the twenty-first century:

- Witnessing and evangelizing worldwide
- Equipping the Church for transforming mission
- Engaging in ministries of reconciliation, justice, healing and grace
- Living the Good News of Jesus Christ in community with people who are poor[10]

Chapter 8

Signs of God's Transformation

Jesus and his disciples had also been invited to the wedding. When the wine gave out, the mother of Jesus said to him, "They have no wine." . . . His mother said to the servants, "Do whatever he tells you." . . . Jesus said to them, "Fill the jars with water." And they filled them up to the brim. . . . When the steward tasted the water that had become wine . . . [he] said to the bridegroom, "Everyone serves the good wine first . . . but you have kept the good wine until now." Jesus did this, the first of his signs, in Cana of Galilee, and revealed his glory; and his disciples believed in him.

—John 2:2–3, 5, 7, 9–11

The first "sign" of Jesus recorded in the Fourth Gospel was the transformation of water into wine. Three signs in John involved healing (4:46–54; 5:1–15; 9:1–41). Another sign was the feeding of the multitude (6:1–14). The raising of Lazarus, the sixth sign (11:1–44), points to the greatest sign, the death and resurrection of Jesus. Like signs along the highway, the signs point to what lies ahead, to God's future. They are demonstrations and anticipations of God's transforming mission that establishes God's realm of life. The signs point to God's glory revealed in Christ and to God's intention to transform death into life, sickness into wholeness, swords into plowshares, sorrow into joy, and want into shared abundance.

The disciples perform no "signs" in John. Only Jesus does. Only God transforms. Only God brings in God's future. God freely calls, saves, and sends. Who transformed the water into wine? Jesus. Who participated in the transformation? Mary told Jesus about the problem: " 'They have no wine.' " Recognizing human limitation and divine sovereignty, Jesus said, " 'Woman, what concern is that to you and to me? My hour has not yet come.' " Divine control does not eliminate responsible human participation. Mary prepared the servants to participate. Jesus asked them to fill the jars and then to serve the steward. Interestingly the disciples did not participate. It was the beginning of their own conversion and process of transformation in preparation for the final commission: "'As the Father has sent me, so I send you'" (John 20:21).

God's Mission Transforms

The *missio Dei* is God's transforming activity in the world. God's mission of forgiveness, restoration, reconciliation, and liberation is continually transforming all engaged in and touched by it. God declares and determines that we "are being transformed into the same image from one degree of glory to another" because "in Christ, there is a new creation" (2 Cor. 3:18; 5:17). We know that through Christ God's plan is to "gather up all things" (Eph. 1:10) and to "reconcile to [God]self all things, whether on earth or in heaven, by making peace through the blood of his cross" (Col. 1:20). Thus, we look forward to God's final intervention and consummation, anticipating "a new heaven and a new earth," where "the river of the water of life" flows and "the tree of life with its twelve kinds of fruit" grows. Indeed, we rejoice and proclaim with thanksgiving, "The leaves of the tree are for the healing of the nations" (Rev. 21:1; 22:1, 2).

However, the empirical reality of violence, war, hunger, disease, greed, and injustice in our world makes it hard to believe that God's mission transforms. Where is God at work? How long will the transformation take? We believe that the triune God of love gives and respects human freedom and dignity. The disgrace in the world is the consequence of humanity's misuse of the freedom God gives. God suffers with the groaning world. God's transforming work is by love, not by force; by invitation, not by demand; by response to the gift of grace, not by manipulation. God is respectful, gracious, and patient. The transforming gospel acts as salt, light, and leaven—impacting society and bringing change, either gradually or suddenly. God's transformation does come, either dramatically or without notice. Every sign of it gives us renewed eschatological hope. What is hidden will surely be revealed in "the fullness of time" (Eph. 1:10).

Mission Is Being Transformed

In his monumental work *Transforming Mission,* David J. Bosch uses "transforming" at two levels. First, God's mission transforms people. This transformation of people is reciprocal, as Christians in one land are transformed by the witness of Christians in other lands. Beyond transforming people, Bosch asserts that at a deeper level our very understanding and practice of mission is being transformed. That is, mission transforms mission. Former mission fields have become mission sending agents. The global church's center of gravity and mission leadership has shifted southward. Consequently, the theology of mission is progressively changing:

> from the church's mission to God's mission (*missio Dei)*
> from "sending" to "being sent"
> from church-focused to kingdom-focused
> from doing "for" to doing and being "with" (solidarity)
> from coming "from above" to coming "from below"
> from mission "out of affluence" to mission "out of poverty"
> from polarization of evangelism and social justice to holistic mission
> from one-way mission to networks and mutual partnerships.[1]

If we were to truly follow these directions, our understanding of and participation in God's transforming mission would be radically transformed. We would perceive the emergence of a new mission paradigm. We would experiment with new roles, attitudes, and practices in our mission partnerships. Though we have been suffering the birth pains of a new model of mutual mission in partnership for half a century, our practice lags behind our rhetoric. While churches around the world have gladly embraced this new approach to mission, churches in the United States often demonstrate denial, reluctance, or deep attachment to comfortable paternalistic mission patterns. In response to the challenge of the cutting edge of mutual partnerships, this book attempts to offer practical guidance and counsel to Presbyterian mission enthusiasts around the world and in local PC(USA) churches who seek more authentic and faithful mission partnerships of mutuality and reciprocity.

God's Mission Transforms Persons, Churches, and Societies

Creation is groaning. We all need to change. What is the scope and nature of the transforming work of God's grace? *Missio Dei* converts and transforms individuals, churches, communities, structures of societies, the world, and all of creation. The opening and closing chapters of the Bible, together with many psalms show how animals, plants, trees, rivers, and mountains are part of the glory of God's mission in worship, praise and proclamation.

Vinay Samuel contends in *Mission as Transformation* that the social dimensions of the gospel are as important as the personal dimensions. Thus, reconciliation, solidarity, and community development are essential components in mission. Samuel defines community building as "total commitment to the social community, to build communities, to build and bring change." He advises mission workers, "You are not there to bring transformation yourself. You are on a journey yourself of self transformation, of community transformation, and you are inviting the people to join a journey, and witness to them of your Lord and your experience."[2] Samuel warns against a "week of mission" divorced from the "costly process" of social and personal transformation "in the long haul." He suggests that "one of the contexts where transformation takes place is where you enable communities and individuals to see God intervene and be present personally and directly, not just in words, but enabling reconciliation to shape community life, so that the relationships of the group that is involved are shaped by reconciliation."[3]

When we understand that transformation and conversion are both personal and social, individual and corporate, there is no longer a debate over the importance or priority of evangelism and social justice. Evangelism, compassionate service, and social justice are all imperative in God's holistic mission. God is continually transforming, converting, and liberating persons, congregations, denominations, communities, and societies. Participation in God's mission both requires and results in personal and corporate lifestyle and worldview changes. Profession of Jesus Christ as one's personal Savior and Lord is the beginning of a life-long transformation of the whole person in all realms of life through discipleship and witness in the context of community.

Presbyterians involved in mission are being transformed in numerous ways, and we trust that other people are being transformed by God because of their lives, witness, teaching, preaching, and healing. The Presbyterian Hunger Program, International Health Ministries, and Self-Development of People Program are all committed to development as transformation. We join in solidarity with partners, including nongovernmental organizations, churches, schools, hospitals, grassroots communities, and governments around the world who seek God's liberating changes and just structures and systems. It is risky to be on the side of God's transformation and to be in solidarity with those who seek it. It is risky because such mission draws us into the struggles of life, fully aware that many lives have been lost along the way.

Retired PC(USA) mission workers Ross and Gloria Kinsler help Christians understand and respond to economic globalization. To address the inequality and injustice that is so blatant in our world's distribution of resources, they turn to the biblical idea of jubilee that promises "fullness of life for all God's people." They make it clear that "enough for all" is "gospel" and offer Jubilee as a model for personal, ecclesial, and social transformation. "Responsible discipleship" begins with repentance. "We must then repent of, reject, and turn away from those policies and decisions that enable our country to continue practicing injustice of all kinds."[4] The Kinslers contrast many of the domination systems and structures in our world with Jesus' power expressed through self-denial and self-giving. No matter how much we agree in principle and even teach that, as a denomination and as mission workers from the United States, we must recognize and admit that "we are bound up in socioeconomic structures and dynamics that benefit us and marginalize others."[5] In other words, the root causes of many of the world's problems and needs involve the structures of our own society. So what is the solution? The Kinslers see a hopeful shape of discipleship in the popular "twelve step" models of recovery. As we seek to move beyond the dominant mission paradigm of Western Christendom and experience new paradigms of partnership, we find ourselves on the road to recovery, dependent on the grace of God every step of the way.

Participation in mission in partnership with the triune God and God's global Church will bring transformation to us, our congregations, our denomination, our society, and our world. We must remember that transformation is not only personal and social, but also ecclesial. Therein, God calls the Church "to a new openness to God's continuing reformation of the Church ecumenical, that it might be a more effective instrument of mission in the world."[6] Furthermore, Philip Wickeri reminds us of the importance of transforming structures of mission and offers the United Church of Christ in the Philippines, the Amity Foundation in China, and the Caribbean and North America Council for Mission (CANACOM) as examples of churches that have created structural changes in their partner relationships and networks.[7] We must subject our mission structures and organizations to the changing winds of God's mission movement. The dynamics and issues in our world and in the global church demand renewed mission structures.

Equipping the Church for Transforming Mission

The call we receive in baptism is to participate in the communion of the Trinity, to be part of the universal church, and to be agents and signs of God's Trinitarian mission of sending, going, receiving, and giving. "All this is from God, who reconciled us to [God]self through Christ, and has given us the ministry of reconciliation; . . . So we are ambassadors for Christ, since God is making [God's] appeal through us" (2 Cor. 5:18, 20).

According to the PC(USA) *Book of Order,* "The Church is called to be a sign in and for the world of the new reality which God has made available to people in Jesus Christ."[8] Furthermore,

    a. The Church is called to tell the good news of salvation by the grace of God through faith in Jesus Christ as the only Savior and Lord, proclaiming in Word and Sacrament that
       (1) the new age has dawned.
       (2) God who creates life, frees those in bondage, forgives sin, reconciles brokenness, makes all things new, is still at work in the world.
    b. The Church is called to present the claims of Jesus Christ, leading persons to repentance, acceptance of him as Savior and Lord, and new life as his disciples.
    c. The Church is called to be Christ's faithful evangelist
       (1) going into the world, making disciples of all nations. . . .
       (2) demonstrating by the love of its members for one another and by the quality of its common life the new reality in Christ. . . .
       (3) participating in God's activity in the world through its life for others by
          (a) healing and reconciling and binding up wounds,
          (b) ministering to the needs of the poor, the sick, the lonely, and the powerless,
          (c) engaging in the struggle to free people from sin, fear, oppression, hunger, and injustice,
          (d) giving itself and its substance to the service of those who suffer,
          (e) sharing with Christ in the establishing of his just, peaceable, and loving rule in the world.[9]

How do we equip one another for these missional tasks?

1. *By sharing best practices.* Missional practices are communal and experiential. Mission workers, congregations, denominational program staff, and other groups share with each other their practices of being evangelized and evangelizing, being healed and healing, and building community and empowering builders. We share our journey to mutuality. We examine our practices to determine if they are clothed in the attitudes of respect, humility, and compassion.

2. *By study and reflection.* Hopefully this book is a useful tool for all persons and churches engaged in God's mission and for Presbyterians seeking to understand and implement the partnership policy statement. The guide at the end and bibliographical sources can facilitate creative reflection by groups and individuals.

3. By gathering as "mission networks" with common mission interests. Networks are the wave in our globalized world and information age. Mission networks are informal collegial partnerships between entities and persons working together or sharing information around specific regions, countries, people groups or programmatic areas of international mission. As information, experience and wisdom are shared, people are better equipped for mission.

4. By worship and thanksgiving. Interestingly, the PC(USA) *Directory of Worship* recapitulates the basic elements of God's transforming mission— Proclamation and Evangelism; Compassion; Reconciliation: Justice and Peace; and Caring for Creation and Life—then moves to the ultimate goal of mission: the Reign of God and God's praise. "In worship the church is transformed and renewed, equipped and sent to serve God's reign in the world. The church looks for the day 'when every knee shall bow, in heaven and on earth and under the earth and every tongue confess that Jesus Christ is Lord, to the glory of God the Father'"(Phil. 2:9–11).[10] Indeed, our praise and proclamation of God's coming reign is a sign and witness that leads to our mutual evangelization and discipleship. The experience of sharing grace, of being adopted by God into the one body of Christ, of participating in and thanksgiving for God's self-giving in the Eucharist renews us for service.

Letting God's Grace Transform Us

Gathering for God's Future ends with "A Renewed Call to Worldwide Mission."

> God offers us an urgent call. It is a call to pray and discern. It is a call to study the most crying needs and the ways God would have us address them. It is a call to let God transform us for our role in the world church for the sake of God's intentions for the world. It is a call to partner with Christians near and far, mobilized as Presbyterians working together worldwide in witness, discipleship and community.[11]

"Let God transform us." Scriptures make it clear that God's transforming activity includes breaking and healing. Jeremiah uses a prophetic parable and analogy that helps us understand this (18:1–12). The prophet goes down to the potter's house and sees the artisan working at his wheel. "The vessel he was making of clay was spoiled in the potter's hand, and he reworked it into another vessel, as seemed good to him" (Jer. 18:4). As individuals, churches, and nations we are spoiled, marred, broken, imperfect vessels of clay that need to be constantly reworked or transformed by the potter. Are we willing to let the potter remake and change us? The prophet suggests that our role is not one of passivity. God's sovereign mission practice allows the freedom of human response and responsibility. God offers grace and forgiveness. God offers restoration for broken vessels. Though marred, we are still created in God's relational image and can respond. Trusting in the One who offers forgiveness that can heal our wounds, we open ourselves to receive God's grace. We expose our wounds and allow God to touch our fragility. We assume a position of vulnerability, receptivity, and brokenness that enables us to experience the realm of God as sheer gift. We admit, accept, and own our limits and sins. We open ourselves to the risk of growth pains and accept God's transformation.

Suddenly we understand Luke's insistence that "repentance and forgiveness of sins is to be proclaimed in [Christ's] name to all nations" (24:47). When we open ourselves to receive the gift of forgiveness, we also open ourselves to all that is spoiled and needs forgiving. The grace we share offers to us the possibility of repentance and transformation. To repent is to break away from or change directions. Repentance is more than verbalizing and feeling bad about our personal and structural sins. It is assuming changed attitudes and acting differently. Back to the potter's house, we hear the gracious invitation: "Turn now, all of you from your evil way, and amend your ways and your doings" (Jer. 18:11). We allow the grace-filled potter to expose, challenge, and break our proud, greedy, and selfish ways and remake us into signs of transformation.

Darrell Guder, in *The Continuing Conversion of the Church,* shows how a missional church engages in a continual process of self-examination and repentance of wrong attitudes and actions. Mission organizations can not be transformed witnesses of the gospel they proclaim without ongoing self-analysis and openness to God's reworking. Mission is a process of perpetual conversion for all involved, a journey of imperfect people on the way to God's reign of justice, peace, and love who invite all to join the journey. As we continue the sojourn with God and God's people in this world, we will constantly be broken, corrected, changed, converted, mended, and healed. We know that mission in partnership is impossible without repentance, healing, and forgiveness. Contemplating our broken selves, churches, and world, we remember the good news of the gospel: in Christ we are forgiven.

Hence, the questions lying at the heart of transforming mission are these: Are we prepared to be changed? Are we open to the Potter's continual breaking and healing? Are we willing to let God's grace transform us? If we are, we are in for a transformational adventure.

Joint Ventures of Grace

As individuals, congregations, organizations, and denominations we find ourselves being converted to God's mission in partnership. Anthony Gittins sees Christian mission as *"the greatest religious adventure"* that "calls us to a triple personal conversion: to God, to culture, and to other people."[12] Our partnership in mission begins when we respond to God's grace and enter into a relationship of gift exchange with God and of sharing grace with others. We become participants in the communion, grace, and mission of the triune God. Could there be a greater adventure?

Mission is movement, coming and going, being sent and receiving. *Missio Dei* pushes us beyond ourselves and our familiar routines. The church exists *toward* and *for* the world. We cross frontiers and barriers and encounter others. Not only are we open to God's grace and our own fragility, but we are challenged to open ourselves to other peoples and cultures and the gifts they offer and God's presence in them. When we courageously surmount our ethnocentrism and egocentrism and embrace the discipline of receptivity, we make countless discoveries—new textures, tastes, shapes, rhythms, customs, and friendships. We are enriched as we discover the cultural treasures dispersed among the nations. Some of us eventually become bicultural or multicultural people, global citizens. We are converted to other ways of thinking and acting. Our ideas and perspectives are turned upside-down and inside-out. We become what Miroslav Wolf calls a "catholic personality," a personality enriched and made more complete by others and by diversity. We discover that we want and need other partners who are different from us. Experimenting newness and moving toward catholicity in the body of Christ become a joyful joint venture of grace.

Mission in partnership is a discipline. Our conversion to partnership leads to the cultivation of the missional attitudes of respect, humility, and compassion. The practice of mission in ways that reflect the dynamics of *mutuality* and *shared grace* stretches us to embrace *both* the roles of observing *and* participating, listening *and* speaking, sharing suffering *and* suffering, sharing joys *and* celebrating, waiting *and* praying, receiving *and* giving, learning *and* teaching, building community *and* empowering builders, receiving witnesses *and* witnessing, being healed *and* healing. By switching roles we stumble upon the surprising adventure of "mission in reverse." We experience mutual correction, mutual encouragement, mutual growth, and mutual renewal. As a result of this partnership adventure and discipline, we are all being transformed by God. Through the synergy of interdependence, our attitudes and practices are being changed.

Mission in partnership is a transformational adventure. We do not realize when we initiate a partnership what kind of dynamic will be unleashed on the journey. Something new will be created that neither partner controls, that neither can anticipate or foresee. We step out in faith with a commitment to interact in a state of release and trust, rather than control and subordination. We are not sure where the partnership will lead us, so we feel vulnerable. We leave our safe haven, edge out of our comfort zone, and make a leap of faith. There is no guarantee of what will happen along the way to God's future. A risk. A discipline. An adventure. Heirs of Christ sharing grace.

In the final analysis, *missio Dei* remains a mystery. "'The wind blows where it chooses, and you hear the sound of it, but you do not know where it comes from or where it goes. So it is with everyone who is born of the Spirit'" (John 3:8). We let go and allow God's grace to sweep us all up together into God's transforming mission and future. God's breath *co*-missions and empowers the community: "'So I send you, . . . Receive the Holy Spirit'" (John 20:21–22). Jesus bids us, "'Follow me'" (John 20:22) to marvelous joint ventures of grace.

Appendix A

A Guide for Group Reflection and Practice

*T*his study guide can be used by group leaders or individuals. May the Holy Spirit use it to enable you and your group to discover and participate in God's transforming mission.

CHAPTER 1—PARTNERSHIP IN MISSION: GOD SENDS THE SON INTO THE WORLD

Opening Images and Questions:

1. What comes to your mind when you hear the word *partnership*? Make a list on the board. Think of (or show or read) a scene from a film, play, book, or poem that exemplifies partnership.

2. How do you like thinking about the Trinity as a *community* or *partnership* of Father, Son, and Spirit in mission? If possible, contemplate Andrei Rublev's marvelous Russian icon of the Holy Trinity from the fifteenth century or other appropriate art or diagrams.

3. What was your overall impression of and personal reaction to the chapter?

Readings and Questions for Reflection:

1. Read and discuss John 4:34–38. The Savior "sent" by God *sends* the disciples into a collaborative endeavor with God and with other human agents. Partnership is *entering into* and *sharing* the work *of others*. What does this mean? How do you feel about entering into the work of others and having others enter into your work? How do you think others feel about your entering into their work? What does it require of both parties? What are the problems, fears, and dangers? How can "sowers and reapers" who are very different or distant "rejoice together"?

2. Jesus uses the metaphors "doing God's work" and "bearing much fruit" to speak of God's mission in which we participate, but he makes it clear that

all the glory belongs to God. We are only obedient instruments. How do we know if mission endeavors today spring from divine or human initiatives and if they seek divine or human glory? Debate these issues.

Missional Practices

1. A key verse in John's Prologue is "And the Word became flesh and lived among us" (1:14). If the incarnation is a key for contextual missionary practice today, what are the implications for churches from rich nations? How do we move beyond our cultural assumptions of superiority and take the time to identify with people of other cultures, religions, and social-economic situations? Give examples of ways that you and your congregation might do this.

2. Read and discuss these passages: John 3:16–17; 4:34; 5:30; 20:21. The whole church is sent into the world as an agent of God's mission. If no individual, committee, or congregation can do God's mission alone, how can we join hands with God and others in mission? Give concrete examples.

3. Read John 12:1–3 and 13:1–15. What are some practical ways that we might follow the examples of Mary and Jesus today, mutually giving and receiving in order to share and serve one another with humble love? Is this possible? Is it easy or hard for you? Why?

Missional Prayer

Close by forming dyads or triads that become "prayer partners." Pray that you will be obedient and attentive followers of Jesus Christ, that God will send you and your church into the world as agents of God's mission, and that you will be open to receive from other instruments of God's mission.

CHAPTER 2—GOD SENDS THE CHURCH INTO THE WORLD IN THE POWER OF THE HOLY SPIRIT

Opening Images and Questions:

1. Place a chalice with wine or grape juice, a loaf of bread, a bunch of grapes, stalks of wheat (if possible), a pitcher with water, and a basin in the center of the room. Go around the group and give everyone a chance to share his or her thoughts and experiences of baptism and the eucharist.

2. When you participate in and reflect on the sacraments, do you perceive that you are united with all baptized children of God everywhere and are partaking of one loaf as a part of one body with Christians of all nations worldwide? Invite the participants to talk about when and why they have this perception or when and why they do not.

Readings and Questions for Reflection:

Divide into four groups or select four individuals to read out loud to the class Jesus' Missionary Prayer in John 17:1–17 and Great Commission in John 20:19–23.

Group 1: Jesus Is Sent—John 17:1–5
Group 2: The Disciples Are Sent—John 17:6–19
Group 3: Sent to Those Who Will Believe—John 17:20–26
Group 4: The Disciples Are Sent—John 20:19–23.

Discuss the following questions.

1. What is the relation between the "sending" of Jesus and the "sending" of the disciples?

2. Where does the "world" into which we are "sent" begin? Define your "mission field." It may be closer than you think. What does it mean to connect mission near and far?

3. What is the importance of unity in and for mission?

4. How do you understand the role of the Holy Spirit in mission today?

Missional Practices

1. What is the practical meaning of having partnerships of love between churches and cultures?

2. Describe all the ways that your local congregation, presbytery, and denomination participate in ecumenical mission.

3. Think of ways that you might practice unity in this class today, in your local congregation, in your town, in your work and ministry, in your denomination, and in wider circles.

4. In groups or as a class, create and present a diagram, chart, work of art with paint or Play-Doh, litany, confession of faith, prayer, liturgical dance, role play, pantomime, drama, or song that demonstrates unity in God's mission.

5. Recite together the Nicene Creed or Apostles' Creed. (Use an overhead projector, Power Point presentation, or photocopy if necessary.)

Missional Prayer

Close by placing the phrase "Send us into the world" and the passage John 17:1–26 on a poster, board, transparency, or slide. Allow members of the class to use spontaneously phrases from the text to formulate their prayers. After each prayer, use as a group response "Send us into the world."

CHAPTER 3—MISSIONAL ATTITUDES: RESPECT

Opening Images and Questions:

1. Present an example of lack of respect in mission by reading a brief portion from a book or showing a clip from a film such as *The Poisonwood Bible* by Barbara Kingsolver, Chinua Achebe's *Things Fall Apart*, Peter Matthiessen's *At Play in the Fields of the Lord*, or James Michener's *Hawaii*. Discuss the following questions: Were the missionaries conscious of their attitude of disrespect? How do you think those whose dignity was disrespected felt?

2. Think of concrete examples of when others might feel they are "invisible" or are treated as "objects" rather than as "subjects" because of our Western culture of domination.

3. How willing are you to engage in self-critique?

Readings and Questions for Reflection:

1. Read John 13:34, 35: "'I give you a new commandment, that you love one another. Just as I have loved you, you also should love one another. By this everyone will know that you are my disciples, if you have love for one another.'" Do you ever feel like this is an impossible ideal or a utopian moral platitude that has lost its meaning? Would it be more attainable to begin with "respect one another"? What is the difference?

2. It says in the chapter that "a challenge for privileged North Americans is learning to show respect for the race, ethnic identity, culture, and nationality of others." How do you feel about this statement? Have you recognized and accepted this challenge? Share your reflections.

3. Reflect on the differences between denominations and world religions today in our pluralistic society. Can you think of ways that disrespect for differences leads to violence and ways that respect for differences leads to peaceful coexistence?

Missional Attitudes and Practices

1. How can mission workers show respect for the partner churches with whom they work?

2. Can you think of ways visiting groups in other countries and cultures can be respectful guests?

3. How do partner churches show respect for the mission workers with whom they work?

4. Have you experienced respect and the recognition of your dignity and worth from a mission partner? Share your experience.

5. If you are involved in a mission partnership individually or collectively

as a congregation, presbytery, or denomination, candidly respond to the following discerning questions the PC(USA) policy statement poses under the principle "Recognition and Respect":

- Is there recognition of the self-affirmed identities of each partner?
- Are the unique contexts of all partners recognized and respected?
- Are gifts and needs of all partners affirmed and respected?
- Are cultural differences being mediated with sincerity and in a Christlike manner?[1]

6. Divide into groups. Plan a short skit or dramatization to present to the class that demonstrates the presence and/or absence of the attitude of respect in mission work.

Missional Prayer

Close with a few minutes of silent reflection for self-critique and identification of your blind spots. Ask God's Spirit to give you the courage and honesty to name and admit your sinful attitudes and to resist attitudes and structures of disrespect. Make a commitment to a "continual conversion toward respect." Begin that journey by praying for one person or group toward whom you need to show respect today or during this week.

CHAPTER 4—MISSIONAL ATTITUDES: COMPASSION

Opening Images and Questions:

1. What comes to your mind when you hear the word *compassion*? Think of (or show or read) a scene from a film, play, book, or poem that exemplifies compassion.

2. When you sense that someone is a compassionate person, what are the traits in that person which lead to this description? Make a list on the board of the traits, elements, or marks of the attitude of compassion.

3. Considering the times compassion is mentioned by the Gospel writers as an attitude that guides Jesus' mission activity, discuss the relevance this has for mission today.

Readings, Dramatizations, and Questions for Reflection:

Divide into two groups and prepare presentations to make to the class:

Group 1: Do a dramatic reading of Luke 10:25–37 with one person as narrator, another as the lawyer, and another as Jesus. Or present a contemporary skit or dramatization of the parable.

Group 2: Do a dramatic reading of Luke 15:11–32 with a narrator, father, younger son, and elder son. Or present a contemporary skit or dramatization of the parable.

Discuss the following questions.

1. It has often been said that we in the church today resemble the priest and Levite in the parable in Luke 10 and the elder brother in Luke 15. What do you think? In what respects does the church resemble the prodigal son? With whom do you identify in these two parables?

2. How is compassion "an intense emotional response"? What does embodiment mean? How do we embody compassion? What does it mean to be relational? How is compassion relational? What did you learn from the compassionate father and Samaritan in the parables?

Missional Attitudes and Practices

1. Can you think of situations in our culture, church, history, or world in which material assistance or aid has been offered without compassion? What concrete suggestions can you give to help your congregation move toward a more compassionate attitude in mission service?

2. It is very difficult for those associated with imperialism to see and learn from the "Samaritans" in the global church today. It is imperative, however, if we want to engage in God's mission in the twenty-first century. Who are the "Samaritans" from whom you have learned? What have you learned from them? What are ways that you could open yourself more to learn from "Samaritans"?

3. Identify and share some of the pain and suffering that you see in your congregation, town or city, country, and world, as well as within yourself. Why do you think we resist emotional reactions and responses to pain? What would it mean for you to respond to the pain of others with compassion? What would it mean for the church to experience God's compassion and "run toward the world in compassion?"

4. What do we need to work on, to cultivate within our being, so that we may one day more truly do mission with the missional attitude of compassion? What can you do today or this week to begin your "continual conversion toward compassion"?

Missional Prayer

Close with a few minutes of silent reflection. Perhaps the most difficult challenge before us is to be open and vulnerable enough to assume the posture of wandering or silent sheep or of prodigal children and admit that very often in our mission partnerships and activities we have not embodied the attitude of compassion. Use the prodigal's prayer, we "have sinned against heaven and before you" and are "no longer worthy to be called" mission partners (Luke 15:6, 7).

CHAPTER 5—MISSIONAL ATTITUDES: HUMILITY

Opening Images and Questions:

1. Place a basin with water and a towel at the center of the room. Display crosses, crucifixes, and works of art that depict the stations of the cross and the passion of Christ. Invite the participants to observe them, to use their imagination, and to comment on the statements in Philippians 2 that Christ Jesus "emptied himself" and "humbled himself."

2. When you sense that someone is a humble person, what are the traits in that person which lead to this description? Make a list on the board of the traits, elements, or marks of the attitude of humility. Then beside each one, place the opposite. Which column sounds more like us?

3. Allow people to share their overall impression of and reactions to the chapter.

Readings and Questions for Reflection:

1. Read Philippians 2:1–13. Note the three occurrences of the word "mind" and discuss what it means for the church today to "let the same mind be in you that was in Christ Jesus."

2. What is the difference between healthy national pride and unhealthy ethnocentrism?

3. What is the difference between evangelistic religious conviction and religious superiority?

4. Motivation, means, interests, and ends are exceedingly complex. To what extent does the significant U.S. military aid to Israel, Egypt, and Colombia serve our "national interests" and to what extent does it serve the interests of the people of those countries? To what extent did the unilateral U.S. military attack on and subsequent nation building in Iraq serve our "national interests" and to what extent did it serve the interests of the people of Iraq? Is it possible to impose democracy by force? Debate these sensitive political issues with a spirit of humility.

Missional Attitudes and Practices

1. Can you think of ways that Christians engaged in mission might unconsciously humiliate others? What concrete suggestions can you give to help your congregation move toward a more humble attitude in mission service?

2. If you are involved in a mission partnership individually or collectively

as a congregation, presbytery, or denomination, candidly respond to the following discerning questions posed by the PC(USA) policy statement under the principle "Shared Grace and Thanksgiving":

- Is there courage to confess human sins and confront the forces which deny the abundant life God promises to all in Jesus Christ?
- Is God's forgiveness mutually shared in Jesus Christ?
- Does the community of partners join in thankful worship to celebrate God's gift of grace and renewal?[2]

3. Continue your analysis of your congregation's mission by discussing these questions:

- Is selfish ambition present in our (my) motives for missional engagement?
- Does our congregation harbor a subtle air of conceit because of our mission budget and projects?

4. Divide into groups. Plan a short skit or dramatization to present to the class that demonstrates the presence and/or absence of the attitude of humility in mission work.

Missional Prayer

Those who are able might get on their knees as a symbol of humility. Let go of entitlement and privilege. Chapters 3, 4, and 5 affirm that mission is not primarily a question of doing but a question of being—a way of living. Reflect on your attitudes. Offer prayers about who you are.

CHAPTER 6—MISSIONAL PRACTICES: OBSERVING AND PARTICIPATING

Opening Images and Observations:

1. Place on tables around the room a wide variety of photographs, magazine pictures, posters, artifacts, and other visual representations of different people, cultures, events, and activities. Give the participants a few moments to walk around and observe them. Allow members to select one and formulate a question they would like to pose to a knowledgeable person that would help them understand more fully what they observed.

2. Ask for a volunteer or two to serve as observers during the class session to observe the participation of all during the class, especially the practice of listening and speaking, and of any of the other practices in the chapter.

3. Go around the circle and share stories of occasions when you partici-

pated in meaningful events or experienced prayer for and worship with other partners in mission.

Listening to God's Word and Reflecting:

1. Read Romans 12:15, "Rejoice with those who rejoice, weep with those who weep," and 1 Corinthians 12:14–26, with emphasis on the last verse: "If one member suffers, all suffer together with it; if one member is honored, all rejoice together with it." What do these passages say to you about mutuality in the body of Christ? In the chapter there are several dyads. Two of them, "sharing sufferings and suffering" and "sharing joys and celebrating," can be placed together to form another dyad. Which of these missional practices is the most difficult for you? Why?

2. Read Acts 1:4–14 and Acts 2:1–13. Comment on the importance of waiting, praying, and worshiping together in the global church's mission today. How can we overcome cultural and linguistic barriers in our mission practices and worship together? What could you do in your congregation to begin overcoming this barrier?

Missional Practices

1. Make a list on the board of the five dyads of mission practices presented in this chapter:

    observing and participating
    listening and speaking
    sharing sufferings and suffering
    sharing joys and celebrating
    waiting and praying

Discuss one at a time how you can apply or implement these in practical ways today. What mission activities do you already practice? Give as many concrete examples as possible. Identify your cutting edges of growth and any new activities or "surprising role reversals" that you need to work on. Talk about how we participate in these mission practices as part of a global community of faith, rather than as individual mission practitioners. Remember ways you have seen your mission partners practice these activities. Show how the dyads pave the road to mutuality.

2. Allow the observer(s) to share their observations about the practice of these missional practices during the class. Then give the class an opportunity to suggest how we might sharpen our practices beginning in the classroom and in the local church and community.

Missional Prayer

Share your joys and concerns. Starting with them, make a list of specific missional prayers and then pray them. Don't forget: *Prayer is mission.*

CHAPTER 7—MISSIONAL PRACTICES: RECEIVING AND GIVING

Opening Images and Observations:

1. Arrange the room and conduct the class in ways that help build community. Sitting in a circle promotes interconnectedness and equal opportunity to be seen and heard. As an opening ritual, go around the circle and offer thanks to God for one gift the community has received from each person. Place a reminder of the presence of God at the center, maybe a candle and a world globe.

2. Pass the following PC(USA) resources around the circle and allow people to look through them and share examples of the practices in the chapter: *Gathering for God's Future: Witness, Discipleship, Community; Faith in Action; Building Community among Strangers; Hope for a Global Future; Turn to the Living God; Congregation-based Health Care; Mission in the 1990s; Mission and Evangelism: An Ecumenical Affirmation (WCC); Book of Order,* G-chap. 3, "The Church and Its Mission," and W-chap. 7, "Worship and the Ministry of the Church in the World."

Listening to God's Word and Reflecting

1. Read John 1:1–18. What does this passage say to you about the divine-human gift exchange? What other texts in John help you to understand the missional practice of giving and receiving? How do you try to respond to the gifts God has given to you? Read the text out loud again, omitting verses 6–8. Does it flow smoothly without these verses? Why do you think the evangelist inserted them here? What does "witness" have to do with gift exchange and response?

2. Read Matthew 16:13–19 and 1 Corinthians 3:5–15. Think about the "building" images. Who builds? What is being built? What do you think was Christ's main concern? What do you think was Paul's? Do Paul's metaphors refer to the corporate community or to the spiritual life of individual believers? What do these texts say to us today? What should we be building?

Missional Practices

1. Make a list on the board of the five dyads of missional practices presented in this chapter:

>   receiving and giving
>   learning and teaching

building community and empowering builders
receiving witnesses and witnessing
being healed and healing

Discuss one at a time how you can apply or implement these in practical ways today. What mission activities do you already practice? Give as many concrete examples as possible. Identify your cutting edges of growth and any new activities or "surprising role reversals" that you need to work on. Talk about how we participate in these mission practices as part of a global community of faith, rather than as individual mission practitioners. Remember ways you have seen your mission partners practice these activities. Show how the dyads pave the road to mutuality.

2. In the chapter it says, "Gift giving can foster the illusion of superiority because it gives power or control to the giver. Gifts usually help but can also humiliate the recipient, who becomes indebted to the giver. This indebtedness creates the possibility of reciprocity and an ongoing relationship. However, when there is no reciprocity, unidirectional giving spawns dependency and resentment." Can you think of any positive or negative examples of this?

Missional Prayer

Close in a literal or symbolic way that further builds community among you. Provide a safe space for people to share their brokenness and wounds. Starting with them, make a list of specific missional prayers and then pray them. Don't forget: Vulnerability precedes healing.

CHAPTER 8—SIGNS OF GOD'S TRANSFORMATION
Opening Creations and Invitation to Transformation:

Gather in a circle. Place a ceramic chalice and pitcher in the center. Pass containers of clay or Play-Doh around the room and invite participants to take some, to play with it and discover something of what it can do, and then to find in their interaction with it a representation of the new mission paradigm that is emerging in the global church and in them. While people are working with the Play-Doh, slowly read Jeremiah 18:1–12; Isaiah 64:8; 45:9–13; Romans 12:1–2, and 2 Corinthians 4:7–10. After some time, ask members to share their creations and thoughts.

Then have everyone raise their creations and pray the following prayer together:

"Creator God, may the transforming power of your gospel be at work in our lives, in the church, and in every country in the world today and always. Amen."

Listening to God's Word and Reflecting

Prepare two handouts, one with a copy of Ephesians 1:1–14 and the other with Colossians 1:1–20. Divide into groups and give one of the handouts to each person in each group.

1. A facilitator asks each person to read the text silently and circle the word or phrase that best describes signs of God's transformation. Allow each person to share with the group what he or she circled and why.

2. Ask people to read the text again and circle all references to "grace." In the book it says that "sharing grace" is the practice of God's mission in partnership. Talk in the group about the connection between sharing grace and mission in partnership.

3. Have someone read the text out loud and ask everyone to circle all references to "thanksgiving." Talk about how "thanksgiving" is part of sharing grace in partnerships.

Missional Practices

1. We equip one another for transforming mission by sharing best practices. Share with each other some of your missional practices and your experiences of mutual practices with partners in mission. Examine your practices to determine if they are clothed in the attitudes of respect, humility, and compassion.

2. The chapter suggests that transformation is personal, ecclesial, and social.

- How are you being transformed? How have you changed as a result of reading this book? Share signs/give examples of personal transformation in your own understanding, attitudes, and practice of mission.
- How is your church being transformed? Share signs/give examples of ecclesial transformation that is occurring or that you pray for in your local congregation or denomination's theology, attitudes, and practice of mission.
- How is your country's culture being transformed? Share signs/give examples of social transformation or systemic changes that you are willing to pray for and be a part of in your government's policies, your culture, and the structures of your society.

Missional Prayer

Close with prayers of thanksgiving. Allow individuals to spontaneously offer phrases that name "signs" of God's transforming activity in our troubled world. After each phrase, the group responds, "Thanks and glory be to God."

PC(USA) Worldwide Ministries Division Resources:

Partnership, Solidarity and Friendship: Transforming Structures in Mission by Phillip L. Wickeri
International Mission Partnership Manual
People, Places and Partnerships (7th reprint)
Reaching Out to You
Gathering for God's Future: Witness, Discipleship, Community
Building Community among Strangers
Hope for a Global Future
Congregation-based Health Care
Mission in the 1990s
Mission and Evangelism: An Ecumenical Affirmation (WCC)
PC(USA) Book of Order, G-chap. 3, "The Church and Its Mission," and W-chap. 7, "Worship and the Ministry of the Church in the World"
"When God's People Travel Together" series:
  Vol. 1, *A Trip Leader's Planning Manual* by Debby Vial
  Vol. 2, *Reflecting and Acting on Mission Team Experiences,* by Barbara Battin
  Vol. 3, *Bible Studies for Mission,* by Alice Winters
Faith in Action: Development Ministries from a Christian Perspective
Turn to the Living God: Evangelism in the Way of Jesus Christ

Case Studies

Case Study 1—Offending Your Hosts

A local congregation of the PC(USA) received an invitation for an intergenerational group to visit and collaborate with a small local Presbyterian congregation in Brazil in a poor neighborhood. Their project was to help in the construction of a simple, two-story church building with three classrooms on the first floor and a fellowship hall on the second floor. The dean of the local Presbyterian seminary and his wife were in the United States studying English, so they generously offered for the group to use their home for sleeping and cooking breakfast and supper. Their son and another young man who worked at the seminary would be the hosts.

A painful incident occurred on the first evening. A few hours after the group of around twelve people arrived, the house was a mess, with sleeping bags and mattresses everywhere. They settled in, took showers (with electric showerheads that heat the water), dried their hair, and had dinner. The excessive use of energy caused a fuse to blow and they were left in the dark. The two Brazilian hosts frantically found a friend who was attempting to solve the problem.

Meanwhile, the group decided that it was time to have their evening devotionals, which they did in English, with flashlights and candles in the dark. The Brazilian hosts were unable to understand and participate, so after a few minutes they abruptly left the room. A bilingual Brazilian who was accompanying the group stopped the devotional and explained that they had offended their Brazilian hosts. Everyone was surprised and perplexed. They always had daily devotionals on mission trips. The PC(USA) mission worker present tried to explain what it means to be a guest in a strange country. The group leader felt guilty and confused. There were some tears. Others were angry at the Brazilian who ended the devotional. No one knew what to do.

The young adults in the group asked permission to go after the Brazilians. They knocked on the door and asked for forgiveness. Language barriers came down; body language took over; they exchanged hugs and experienced the joy of reconciliation. Soon the fuse was replaced and the lights returned. The rest of the evening was spent in fun, getting to know the hosts.

After this, the leaders decided that there would be no more "English only" devotionals. Actually, there were no more devotionals. Instead, every evening they had informal, bilingual interaction with youth from a local Presbyterian church near the seminary. There was lots of coming and going with games, cards, music, and food. Several evenings the young people in the group went bowling with the Brazilians or to the mall. Everything happened spontaneously.

This was quite a change from their usual mission trips. Some of the adults had doubts about all the unstructured recreation time, the unsupervised youth activities with the Brazilian youth, and no devotionals. There were bilingual prayers before lunch at the construction site and two very meaningful worship services at the church.

Questions for Reflection

1. Why was the bilingual Brazilian so concerned when the hosts left the room?
2. What do you see as the basic issue(s) in the case?
3. The incident resulted in the abandonment of the custom of daily devotionals in English. Do you agree with that? What would you have done?
4. Comment on the presence or absence of the attitudes of respect, compassion, and/or humility.
5. What North American cultural characteristics do you see in this situation? Are they problems? Do any of the dyads of missional practices give us some concrete ways of seeing our own cultural traits and relating in a different way? What practices would you suggest for the group?

Case Study 2—"White Noise"

One day during their mission service with the United Church of Christ in the Philippines (UCCP), Tom and Carol Montgomery-Fate set out on a two-day trip to the village of Mamalao to visit the twelve families who lived there. It was part of their ongoing orientation program to help them understand the culture. On the second day Tom realized they had made the mistake of heading out without their rain ponchos during typhoon season. They took a jeep to the end of the road and were one hour into the final half-day hike when the rains started. There was no choice but to slush through the rain and follow their guide, Modesto, a Philippine community organizer who accompanied them and took care of all their provisions and transportation. Needless to say, it was a messy trip.

When they finally reached the village, they found refuge in a bamboo chapel with a metal roof. They rested and shouted to one another over the downpour. Modesto smiled as he pointed to the roof and said, "White man's noise." Later Modesto explained that a white missionary who visited the community gave the chapel roof as a gift. He was not being critical. Some people were proud of their different kind of roof. Tom, however, realized that "given the choice . . . the people of Mamalao might have spent the money differently, perhaps for rice seedlings to plant on the terraces they had just started on the mountain."[1]

Before falling asleep that night, as Tom reviewed the events of the day, his mind went back to the "white noise" of the roof. In the silence, lying on the floor of the bamboo hut, he imagined a church service going on during one of the frequent Philippine rains and reflected on the disadvantages of a metal roof and the advantages of a thatched bamboo roof. Not only was the latter quieter, but it was also cooler. Though a metal roof would last longer, bamboo was a common and abundant local material, and thatched roofs were easy to construct. Suddenly Tom realized that "a good-hearted outsider had unknowingly misread the culture in an attempt to help." Then he did a bit of self-analysis: " I knew that I did the same thing in Laoag. I seldom knew for sure what to give or how to receive, or what I had *already* given and received."[2]

Soon after Carol and Tom returned to their base in Laoag, they attended a church's elementary school graduation and following the ceremony, a member said, "We really need a new roof." Tom immediately went into a long explanation about the UCCP partnership policy that did not allow mission coworkers to fund projects. Later he realized that he had been hypocritical, and that his method of assuming control and doing all the talking contradicted his message. He concluded,

Both "worlds" need to relearn how to give and receive the gifts of their cultures. . . . One key to struggling with the Two-Thirds World toward partnership, is for us in the One-Third World to learn how to wait and listen. This is perhaps the greatest gift we can give. Waiting and listening are necessary if we are to learn how to receive the gifts of our partner cultures. But if they don't speak, or if we don't hear the voices, it may mean patiently listening to silence. . . . If we wait long enough and listen hard enough, we will gain the capacity to hear new voices emerge from our white noise.[3]

Questions for Reflection

1. How could attentive listening help avoid misreading or ignoring other cultures?
2. How do our excessive activities, words, structures, and resources become "white noise"?
3. Are good intentions enough in mission giving? Did the missionary make a mistake? How would you have responded to the member's request if you were Tom?
4. Comment on the presence or absence of the attitudes of respect, compassion, and/or humility.
5. Who are the principal characters in the case? What are the missional practices of each? What does it mean to wait and listen? How essential are role reversals today in order to practice the dynamic of mutuality in listening and speaking and in giving and receiving? Which practices are harder for you?

Case Study 3—What is the Global Crisis?

Dr. Elsa Tamez, Professor of the Latin American Biblical University in Costa Rica, told the PC(USA) in an interview, "The attack on the World Trade Center Towers and the Pentagon is made to seem as if the urgent problem today is international terrorism, but the majority of the world is suffering daily deaths because of malnutrition and sickness." She tells us, "I think this is an historic chance for the church to give its prophetic word and to recuperate its credibility in many circles. For this we need profound preparation and much courage."

Our government's response to the tragedy was a preventive attack on Iraq and the removal of Saddam Hussein. Dr. Tamez was so disappointed with the U.S. government's aggressive unilateral response and refusal to work through the United Nations that she has refused to accept invitations to teach and speak in the United States. The justifications for the war—the accusations of chemical and biological weapons of mass destruction, uranium from Africa for nuclear weapons, and connections with Bin Laden and Al-Qaeda have since been questioned. Many U.S. lives have been lost in the aftermath. During the rebuilding of Iraq, the PC(USA) has attempted to reach out and help Iraq's children, especially those in high-poverty areas. Sometimes this is difficult because the U. S. military is controlling most of the relief effort. The PC(USA) joined other churches in requesting that the United Nations, member states, and NGOs (nongovernmental organizations) be entrusted with this responsibility.

Though attention today is focused on Iraq and Israel/Palestine, our "war" on drugs in Colombia has moved to a new level of involvement. The U.S. government's policy now permits our $104 million in military foreign aid to the Colombian drug war to allow U.S.-donated equipment to be used not only to destroy drugs but also directly against the rebels. PC(USA) mission worker Alice Winters tells of those who criticize our military aid and claim that it further fuels the violence and funds human rights violations.

Our partner churches and ecumenical leaders declare that the most serious crisis countries in South America face is neither warfare, drugs, nor natural disaster. People are suffering because of economic problems, such as huge foreign debts, unequal income distribution, and economic globalization that "contributes to dismantling rather than sustaining community. People are not only suffering, they are being systemically excluded from the community."[4] In other words, poverty and sickness are caused by economic problems with foreign roots.

Questions for Reflection:

1. How do history, U.S. interventions, and military aid cause unseen barriers in partnerships? Can you understand our international partners' perspectives and reactions to U.S. foreign policy? What would it mean for us to assume the attitudes of humility and respect in global relationships and to concentrate on the practices of listening and learning when partners express opinions on U.S. foreign policy?
2. What do you see as the basic issue(s) in the case?
3. What appeared a few decades ago to be generous "development aid" through loans to South American nations is now a nightmare because, though the principal has been paid several times, the interest is overwhelming. When is material assistance helpful and when is it harmful? What is our responsibility for the economic situation in Latin America? What should we do?
4. Can we share the suffering of the people where we go in mission knowing that we benefit from the economic system and/or military policy that causes their suffering?
5. What missional practices might your congregation engage in to bring social and structural transformation in the U.S. culture and government?

Case Study 4—Receiving and Giving Is Complicated

After several exploratory visits and a time of getting to know one another and praying for one another, a presbytery of the PC(USA) entered into a formal partnership agreement with a presbytery in South America to be evaluated after five years. A PC(USA) mission couple served as the partnership facilitators. The Latin presbytery presented a project to build a wing of educational classrooms beside one of their congregations to serve as a Sunday School and as a public primary school during the week in partnership with the local government. The project further included a small building for a day clinic in another town where two congregations were located. The U.S. presbytery found the needs compelling. A small delegation visited the sites. In dialogue they agreed to raise the funds. Twenty PC(USA) congregations got involved.

Members of the South American presbytery were invited to visit their partner in the North. One pastor in the delegation was given an opportunity to speak for five minutes in a presbytery mission conference. Those who attended gained a new way of understanding Scripture "from below" and a different perspective on world events. Many of them were moved and challenged. However, some were angry and thought the pastor was "meddling" and had strange hermeneutics. The short presentation generated much discussion and debate. A few people walked out because they had a hard time understanding his English.

The mission enthusiasts in one of the congregations in the PC(USA) presbytery decided to invite a layperson from their partner presbytery to come to the United States and spend six weeks in the Mission to the U.S.A. program. She participated in many of the church's programs and events and shared her testimony. They were blessed by her courageous Christian values and the beauty of the artwork used in her presentations. The members offered many gifts to her when she left to share with her family and congregation. They wanted to maintain a relationship with her and promised to keep in touch by letters and e-mail. Periodically, they would receive requests for financial help to which they responded generously. Some of them began to notice that the requests were more frequent and for considerable sums.

In a return visit to South America, members of the PC(USA) were overwhelmed with the warm hospitality they received from the people in the congregations. They had few material resources, but were so generous and welcoming. The "wealth gap" between the two presbyteries was blatantly apparent, sometimes disturbing. Some of the members had feelings of guilt. In conversations with the partners through translators, they received tremendous inspiration. Their priorities and spirituality were challenged when they saw the peace, joy, deep faith, and genuine dependence of the people upon God. Some of the group spent a few days with sisters and brothers who were suffering in unjust land struggles and joined them in a peaceful demonstration. It was scary, but exciting. Others visited the two construction projects and joined in painting the new day clinic. When they asked about equipment and staff to maintain the clinic, there were no clear answers. The PC(USA) mission couple mentioned the possibility of presenting a new project request. They visited one doctor in a very busy hospital in town who was willing to help during her free time. On the last day of the visit, the Latin presbytery presented a project for building a large church sanctuary in another town where they wanted to begin a new evangelistic field (new church development) and a project for equipping two other churches with new pews and pulpits. Furthermore, they requested scholarship aid for three young people who felt God's call to go to seminary. One Latin American pastor in the presbytery made the comment, "We will be happy to receive whatever you want to give."

Questions for Reflection

1. How, through our partnerships, can our folks encourage a greater understanding of the issues involved as they discuss projects with their international partners? How might the partners deal with projects, requests, and fund-raising in a way that avoids the long tradition of paternalistic gift giving that creates financial dependencies and harmful greed?
2. How do partnerships become truly "mutual"? How does the two-way dimension occur? What is the role of the national leadership in each of the partner churches in equipping their own leadership to understand the issues?
3. Comment on the presence or absence of the attitudes of respect, compassion, and/or humility.
4. What does each partner give and receive in this mission partnership? Are there any conflicting messages? How could the partnership mature to become a more authentic mutual gift exchange?

Case Study 5—Transforming Mission

A PC(USA) mission coworker was invited to teach in a seminary of a partner church, the Independent Presbyterian Church of Brazil. This denomination was started in 1903 by a group who left the Presbyterian Church of Brazil. One of the main reasons was that they did not agree with the control and educational policies of the Presbyterian missionaries from the United States. They wanted to be an autonomous church, free from foreign control or manipulation. After seventy-five years of existence as a truly Brazilian denomination, in 1978 they decided that both their denomination and the PC(USA) had matured to the point of entering into a partnership of mutuality.

The missionary professor was aware of this history and of a certain anti-

Americanism in the denomination. In conversations with faculty and students she gradually learned to engage in mutual criticism and correction. Honest dialogue led her to the painful recognition of her blind spots as a North American. Eventually she adopted a posture of repentance for wrong attitudes and practices present in much of the North American missionary work in the Southern Hemisphere. She recognized the fact that our mistakes have resulted in much "internalized oppression," resentment, and hostility on the part of those who have not been treated with dignity and respect. Some of the most difficult lessons she learned became life-long challenges and goals: for example, how to recognize and move beyond arrogance and an attitude of superiority to a spirit of humility while teaching and learning; how to have patience in learning and teaching; how to depend on others in a spirit of vulnerability and need; and how to overcome individualism and isolationism in order to build a global community of teachers and learners. It was a time of intense personal growth, of radical "conversion" to the Brazilian church's perspective, and of struggle to understand the Brazilian context more fully, as well as the beginning of a new missiology.

The professor became a passionate member of the steering committee responsible for transforming the traditional missionary structure into a three-way partnership. The PC(USA), the Independent Presbyterian Church of Brazil (IPIB), and the United Presbyterian Church of Brazil (IPU) joined to form a new mission structure, the Presbyterian Mission of Brazil. The three denominations were members and equal partners in mission. Under the old structure, all the missionaries from the PC(USA) were members and made many decisions about work and funds. While the new structure was designed primarily to be a forum for missiological discussion and an umbrella for legal presence in the country, there were still issues related to the old problem of "control" to be worked out along the way. For example, the participation of ordained persons in Brazilian presbyteries and the perennial problem of projects and transferral of funds from the North to the South without distorting the nature of the relationship.

At the organizational meeting of the Presbyterian Mission of Brazil, the missionary professor received criticism and even opposition from some of her missionary colleagues. With suspicion and a bit of jealousy, they perceived her as a kind of threat or traitor who was giving up too much power to the Brazilian churches that meant a loss of control by the missionaries. They would no longer be at the center of the flow of information and funds. It was a major transition that produced a missionary identity crisis. The nature of the relationships with the Independent Presbyterian Church of Brazil and the United Presbyterian Church of Brazil would be radically different from the former one with the Presbyterian Church of Brazil. The professor was caught between a rock and a hard place. Her identification with her Brazilian colleagues in the newer denominations was great. She loved working with them as equals. She also treasured her missionary colleagues and wanted to maintain her relationship and service together with them.

Questions for Reflection

1. Why is it important to understand church-to-church history? In Brazil, how does the church's history with the U.S. church inform their perspective on mutuality? What happens if people on the Brazilian or U.S. sides do not know the history of the relationship and repeat the mistakes of the past? Working with a partner church after seventy-five years of autonomy, what should mission workers do if they see presbyteries and pastors from North or South either encouraging or going along with the very practices that caused the Brazilian church to declare its independence?
2. What do you think were some of the missionary professor's "blind spots" as a person from a dominant culture and country? Are you vulnerable enough to discover your "blind spots"?
3. Are you prepared for every person you encounter in the host country to be your teacher? Do you believe that there is something you can learn from each one? Do you have a teachable spirit?
4. How does the history of mission structures affect perspectives, fears, concerns, and expectations? Imagine yourself to have been present at the organizational meeting of the new mission structure. What would you say to the professor and to her colleagues? If you were a mission worker in this situation, what would your position be?

Case Study 6—Disaster Assistance and Community

After a devastating earthquake destroyed hundreds of homes, clinics, churches, and schools, an ecumenical partner organization in Central America invited the PC(USA) to join them in disaster assistance and reconstruction. One presbytery decided to organize five groups to respond. Appeals were made to each congregation in the presbytery. Clothes, blankets, mattresses, food staples, bottled water, medications, medical supplies, Spanish Bibles, bicycles, school supplies, and construction materials were donated generously. Each group had persons with construction, electrical, and medical skills, as well as lots of people with goodwill. They loaded everything up and headed down to Central America to spend three weeks.

When each group arrived at their designated location, they immediately attempted to take control of the situation and systematically distributed the goods. There was a good bit of disorganization and confusion. In some instances there was little or no communication with the organization that extended the invitation. The group leaders tried to impose some kind of order. When word spread that they had food and goods, long lines quickly formed. Folks were happy to receive all assistance that was offered, without asking any questions. However, some of the clothing and food items were strange and ended up being discarded. There was a great deal of efficiency and little time for relationships and conversations. The medical personnel worked long hours. Those assigned to cleanup and building joined local church groups and service organizations involved in this work, sometimes following them, sometimes taking over. Language barriers and diverse styles of leadership and organization made things difficult.

The American cultural traits of "get it done" and "fix it" were a dominant tone for most members of the groups. The focus was on tasks, and some were endless. The devastating situation was overwhelming, so people tended to keep busy in order not to deal with the difficult emotional aspects. Occasionally people simply broke down into tears. It was hard to stop and have time for relationships or emotions. It was hard to imagine the psychological trauma and stress of the local people whose lives had been suddenly disrupted. Even recreation and worship seemed inappropriate under the circumstances. After the three weeks, everyone was exhausted. All the goods had been distributed. There was still so much to be done. Some friendships began to blossom. They wondered if they would ever see those friends again.

Questions for Reflection

1. What do you see as the basic issue(s) in the case?
2. In these days of decentralization and grassroots initiative, is it essential for local congregations and presbyteries to seek denominational coordination in disaster assistance and other projects? Why or why not? What role might the denominational mission society play in this scenario?
3. What kind of mission training do groups involved in disaster assistance and building projects need? How might they receive training in some of the important missional practices?
4. How might the cross-cultural dynamic at work here affect the experience? Can you see any possible dangers or problems in this kind of project?
5. Imagine what the project would look like being done with the attitudes of respect, compassion, and humility and what the project would look like being done without these attitudes. How would practicing these attitudes result in a more mutual relationship and action?
6. How could this project serve to build community, heal brokenness, and empower builders?

Case Study 7—Cross-cultural Perspectives

A PC(USA) seminary offered a Doctor of Ministry course on Solidarity and Mutuality: a New Paradigm for Mission and Evangelism. The premise of the course was that the church today needs to move beyond all paternalism, cultural invasion, imposition, and indifference and embrace the ideals of solidarity and mutuality in global mission. The participants first met in the classroom in the United States for five days for missiological reflection and preparation. Then the group spent ten days in Havana, Cuba, where they were challenged to engage in respectful interaction as observer-participants. They were hosted by the PC(USA) partner church, the Presbyterian Reformed Church of Cuba. They were blessed by the warm hospitality they received from people with very limited access to material resources. They were impressed by the high educational and theological level of all the people they met.

The moving morning worship service at the host Luyano Presbyterian Reformed Church inspired all of them. A young laywoman assisted the pastor, the Rev. Carlos Ham, who was a team teacher of the course. She asked if there were any prayer requests. After a few minutes of silence, one by one at least twenty people—women and men, young and old—came to the microphone and shared requests or answers to prayers. Some were for personal needs, for families, for married couples, for the youth, for the church's planning process, or for victims of the earthquake in Colombia. One woman gave a testimony to answered prayers in her ministry of visiting the sick. When everyone finished, the pastor read a few more requests and then had a prayer that specifically mentioned nearly every request. This church takes prayer seriously.

The students visited the Martin Luther King Center, started by a Baptist church and now a NGO. Alejandro, a Catholic from Argentina, received them, answered questions, and then showed them around. The center offers theological courses and popular education and partners with people in community building and in providing affordable housing. Later the group visited one of the housing projects.

The group heard testimonies of church leaders whose dialogues with President Castro resulted in new freedom, openness, and opportunities for Christian communities. They talked with Christian congress members who believe that socialism is more biblical than other economic systems. They heard theologians give profound lectures on mission and the reign of God. They visited a lay training school and a seminary.

When asked if they could be in solidarity and experience mutuality as denominations, a Cuban theologian answered, "Yes, if two conditions are met: 1) if you protest against and help lift the immoral embargo of the U.S.A. which adversely affects many innocent people in Cuba; and 2) if you provide opportunities in the U.S.A. for your sisters and brothers in Cuba to share what we believe and have experienced. We have highly trained writers, educators, and theologians whose input could be profitable. Why don't U.S. Presbyterians ask for Cuban missionaries for a certain time, and then Cubans will ask for missionaries from the U.S. for a time? After these steps, then we can move forward in mutuality to the sharing of ideas, programs, and human resources."

Questions for Reflection

1. How does history affect our perspectives, fears, and expectations in mission? What is the role that U.S.-to-Cuba history plays in our differing perspectives? Why are visitors often surprised by their international partners' perspectives and reactions to U.S. foreign policy?

2. The cross-cultural dimension of partnership interactions has to do with learning to see and hear a situation from another's perspective. It requires the listening skill of "suspending judgment" until one can grasp the perspective of another. How might the attitudes of humility and respect help us to understand those who favor socialism and help them to see our perspective in a new way?

3. Within partnerships the purpose is a greater witness to Christ, the building up of the church universal, and the demonstration of the values of the peaceful realm of God on earth. What concrete practices might allow our partners and us to check our understandings of the other's perspective and then move forward together for the greater glory of God?

4. What can we learn from our brothers and sisters in Cuba?

5. How can we join the Presbyterian Reformed Church in Cuba in the struggle to lift the embargo and normalize U.S. relations with the island?

Appendix C

"Presbyterians Do Mission in Partnership" Policy Statement[1]

Summary

As heirs to God's grace in Jesus Christ, and joint heirs with all who confess him Lord, we affirm our place as Presbyterians in the whole Body of Christ, the Church.

We understand "Mission" to be God's work for the sake of the world God loves. We understand this work to be centered in the Lordship of Jesus Christ and made real through the active and leading power of the Holy Spirit. Recognizing our human limitations and because of our fundamental unity in Jesus Christ, we believe we are called to mission through the discipline of partnership.

The practice of partnership guides our whole connectional church. It guides us individually as members, officers, and pastors. It guides us collectively as congregations, presbyteries, synods, General Assembly ministries, and related institutions.

In doing mission in partnership, we seek to be guided by certain principles:

1. Shared Grace and Thanksgiving.
2. Mutuality and Interdependence.
3. Recognition and Respect.
4. Open Dialogue and Transparency.
5. Sharing of Resources.

Statement

As heirs to God's grace in Jesus Christ, and joint heirs with all who confess him Lord, we affirm our place as Presbyterians in the whole Body of Christ, the Church. We give visible recognition of our belonging to one another as one denominational family. We give this recognition as Presbyterians through our connectional system of congregations, presbyteries, synods, General Assemblies, and related institutions. The one table around which we gather is God's table and the one mission to which we are called is God's mission.[2]

The Presbyterian Church (USA) declares that wherever one part is engaged in God's mission, all are engaged.[3] Whenever and wherever one engages in that mission, one bears witness to the saving love of God in Jesus Christ. Through this love, empowered by the Holy Spirit, all are made one. This unity is a gift of God's grace that extends across cultural, linguistic, economic and other barriers that divide us within the Body of Christ and across the human family.

Mission

As Christians, we understand "Mission" to be God's work for the sake of the world God loves. We understand this work to be centered in the Lordship of Jesus Christ and made real through the active and leading power of the Holy Spirit. The "where" and "how" and "with whom" of mission is of God's initiative, sovereign action, and redeeming grace. The message we are called to bear is the Good News of salvation through Jesus Christ.

The PC(USA) claims responsibility for bearing the Good News in this way: "The Church is called to be Christ's faithful evangelist

(1) going into the world, making disciples of all nations, baptizing them in the name of the Father and of the Son and of the Holy Spirit, teaching them to observe all he has commanded;

(2) demonstrating by the love of its members for one another and by the quality of its common life the new reality in Christ; sharing in worship, fellowship, and nurture, practicing a deepened life of prayer and service under the guidance of the Holy Spirit;

(3) participating in God's activity in the world through its life for others by
   (a) healing and reconciling and binding up wounds,
   (b) ministering to the needs of the poor, the sick, the lonely, and the powerless,
   (c) engaging in the struggle to free people from sin, fear, oppression, hunger, and injustice,
   (d) giving itself and its substance to the service of those who suffer,
   (e) sharing with Christ in the establishing of his just, peaceable, and loving rule in the world."[4]

Partnership

As Presbyterians, we recognize the Reformed tradition as one part of the larger Body of Christ, the Church. Other communions in the household of God have equally unique and valued places at the table of God's mission. Recognizing our human limitations and because of our fundamental unity in Jesus Christ, we believe we are called to mission in the discipline of partnership. We believe that doing mission in partnership broadens our awareness of how interconnected God's mission is at the local, national and global levels.

Jesus invites us as friends to follow his commandment of love and bear fruit that will last (John 15:12–17). Like Paul and Titus, we become partners with each other and with Christ in united and mutual service (2 Corinthians 8:16–24). Guided by Christ's humility, we work to empty ourselves of all pride, power, sin, and privilege so that God may be glorified (Philippians 2:5–11). Within and beyond our connectional community, doing mission in such true partnership opens us to opportunities for mutual encouragement, mutual transformation, mutual service, and mutual renewal.

The practice of partnership guides our whole connectional church. It guides us individually as members, officers, and pastors. It guides us collectively as congregations, presbyteries, synods, General Assembly ministries, and related institutions. Through prayer, humility and a mutual openness to one another, we develop a cooperative witness that exalts the Lord we serve.

The discipline of partnership assumes that mission can best be done by joining hands with those who share a common vision. Partnership in mission involves two or more organizations who agree to submit themselves to a common task or goal, mutually giving and receiving and surrounded by prayer so that God's work can be more faithfully accomplished. Theologically and biblically, partnership is based on the fundamental belief that God's love for the world is greater than any one church can possibly comprehend or realize.

Knowing the breadth of God's love for the world, we affirm that there are different forms of partnership with different patterns of cooperation. We may join around a common goal with other churches, with secular organizations, or with other faith communities. In any case, work for the common good extends partnership—and the service of God's mission—to all people.

Principles of Partnership

In doing mission in partnership, we seek to be guided by certain principles:

1. **Shared Grace and Thanksgiving.** Partnership *calls* all partners to confess individual and collective failings, to seek forgiveness for complicity

with powers of injustice, to repent from histories of shared exploitation, to move toward common celebration of Christ's sacrifice of reconciliation, and together to give thanks and praise to God for all gifts of grace and renewal.

2. **Mutuality and Interdependence.** Partnership *calls for* interdependence in which mutual aid comes to all, where mutual accountability resides, and no partner dominates another because of affluence or "expertise."

3. **Recognition and Respect.** Partnership *calls* all partners to respect other partners in Christ, and to recognize one another's equal standing before God.

4. **Open Dialogue and Transparency.** Partnership *calls for* open dialogue where a common discernment of God's call to mission is sought, where Scripture is the base for prophetic challenge, where local initiative is respected, where differences are meditated in a Christ-like manner, and where all partners are transparent with regard to their activities and support.

5. **Sharing of Resources.** Partnership *calls for* the sharing of all types of resources: human, cultural, financial and spiritual; especially including friendly conversation and faith-transforming life experiences.

Partnership Commitments

Doing mission in partnership, we commit to be guided by these principles both individually and collectively. In the spirit of candid evaluation, we commit to asking ourselves discerning questions. For each principle, certain approaches are suggested:

1. **Shared Grace and Thanksgiving.**
   - Is there courage to confess human sins and confront the forces which deny the abundant life God promises to all in Jesus Christ?
   - Is God's forgiveness mutually shared in Jesus Christ?
   - Does the community of partners join in thankful worship to celebrate God's gift of grace and renewal?

2. **Mutuality and Interdependence.**
   - Is each partner's self-reliance affirmed, with mutual giving and receiving?
   - Is there space for all partners to be guided by self-determination?
   - Beyond unhealthy dynamics of power and dependency, is there openness to new dynamics of mutual service and mutual renewal?

3. **Recognition and Respect.**
   - Is there recognition of the self-affirmed identities of each partner?

- Are the unique contexts of all partners recognized and respected?
- Are gifts and needs of all partners affirmed and respected?
- Are cultural differences being mediated with sincerity and in a Christ-like manner?

4. **Open Dialogue and Transparency.**
   - Is there local initiative in mission discernment and mission activity?
   - Does God's Word shape us to lovingly confront one another's failings and prophetically challenge the world's systems of power and domination?
   - Is there transparency with all partners about what is being done in mission, even if there is disagreement?

5. **Sharing of Resources.**
   - Do partners minister to and inspire one another, listen to and critique one another?
   - Is there mutual accountability in the exchange of all resources, including human, cultural, financial and spiritual?
   - In trusting relationship, have partners moved beyond two-way relationships into open mission networks and ever-expanding webs of mission relationships?

As heirs to God's grace in Jesus Christ and joint heirs with all who confess him Lord, we commit to wrestle with these questions. We look toward the promise of Christ. We count on the subtle power of the Holy Spirit to guide and limit us. We hope, standing firm in common praise to the triune God, that our practice of partnership may be transformed; that our participation in the *Missio Dei* may more fully contribute to the abundant life that God promises all people and all creation.

Notes

FOREWORD

1. *The Constitution of the Presbyterian Church (U.S.A.)*, part 2, *Book of Order* (Louisville, Ky.: Office of the General Assembly, 2002), G-4.0202–4.0203.

2. Frederick Buechner, *Wishful Thinking: A Theological ABC* (New York: Harper & Row, 1973), 95.

PART 1: WHY? BIBLICAL AND THEOLOGICAL FOUNDATIONS OF PARTNERSHIP

1. J. Andrew Kirk, *What Is Mission? Theological Explorations* (Minneapolis: Fortress Press, 2000), 187.

2. David J. Bosch, *Transforming Mission* (Maryknoll, N.Y.: Orbis Books, 1991), 392.

3. Gustavo Gutiérrez, *The God of Life*, trans. Matthew J. O'Connell (Maryknoll, N.Y.: Orbis Books, 1998), 2.

CHAPTER 1: GOD SENDS THE SON INTO THE WORLD

1. Gustavo Gutiérrez, *The God of Life*, trans. Matthew J. O'Connell (Maryknoll, N.Y.: Orbis Books, 1998), 81.

2. Jürgen Moltmann, *The Trinity and the Kingdom*, trans. Margaret Kohl (Minneapolis: Fortress Press, 1993), 64.

3. Lucien Legrand, *Unity and Plurality: Mission in the Bible*, trans. Robert R. Barr (Maryknoll, N.Y.: Orbis Books, 1990), 134.

4. J. Andrew Kirk, *What Is Mission? Theological Explorations* (Minneapolis: Fortress Press, 2000), 39.

5. Gutiérrez, *The God of Life*, 85.

6. Mortimer Arias and Alan Johnson, *The Great Commission: Biblical Models for Evangelism,* (Nashville: Abingdon Press, 1992), 91.

7. Ibid., 92.

8. Ibid., 93.

9. Raymond Brown, *The Gospel according to John I–XII* (AB 29; New York: Doubleday, 1966), 183.

10. Andreas J. Köstenberger, *The Missions of Jesus & The Disciples according to the Fourth Gospel* (Grand Rapids: Wm. B. Eerdmans Publishing Co., 1998), 183.

11. Interestingly, ancient manuscripts differ over the pronouns. For "we" some read "I" and for "me" some read "us." This discrepancy serves to prove our point, that both Jesus and the disciples are "sent" to engage in God's mission work.

12. Köstenberger, *Missions of Jesus & The Disciples*, 217.

13. Lesslie Newbigin, *The Light Has Come* (Grand Rapids: Wm. B. Eerdmans Publishing Co., 1982), 183.

14. Ibid., 183–84.

15. While the parallel accounts of this story in Mark 14:3–9 and Luke 7:36–50 differ in details, and there are various ideas about who Mary is, John obviously links the story to the family home in chapter 11. The important thing is the lessons we learn from the story and not the details.

16. Raymond Brown, *The Gospel according to John XIII–XXI* (AB 29A; New York: Doubleday, 1970), 565.

CHAPTER 2: GOD SENDS THE CHURCH INTO THE WORLD

1. Jürgen Moltmann, *The Trinity and the Kingdom*, trans. Margaret Kohl (Minneapolis: Fortress Press, 1993), 90.

2. Quoted from Karl Barth, *Church Dogmatics*, in *Transforming Mission*, David J. Bosch (Maryknoll, N.Y.: Orbis Books, 1991), 372.

3. Ibid., 373.

4. Darrell Guder, ed., *Missional Church*, (Grand Rapids: Wm. B. Eerdmans Publishing Co., 1998), 161.

5. Anthony J. Gittins, *Bread for the Journey* (Maryknoll, N.Y.: Orbis Books, 1993), 31.

6. Ibid., 34.

7. Raymond Brown, *The Gospel according to John I–XII* (AB 29; New York: Doubleday, 1966), 293, 292.

8. *The Constitution of the Presbyterian Church (U.S.A.), Part II, Book of Order* (Louisville, Ky.: Office of the General Assembly, 2001), W-7.1000.

9. Ibid., G-3.0200a.

10. Leonardo Boff, *A Trindade e a Sociedade*, Collection Teologia e Libertação, Series II: O Deus Que Liberta seu Povo, 5th ed. (Petropolis: Vozes, 1999), 16.

11. *Book of Order*, G-4-0200.

12. See my article "Local-Global Mission: The Cutting Edge," *Missiology* 28, no. 2 (April 2000): 187–97.

13. See Robert Schreiter, *The New Catholicity: Theology between the Global and the Local* (Maryknoll, N.Y.: Orbis Books, 1997).

14. Boff, *A Trindade*, 192.

CHAPTER 3: RESPECT

1. Shirley C. Guthrie, *God for the World—Church for the World: The Mission of the Church in Today's World* (Louisville, Ky.: Witherspoon Press, 2000), 34.

2. Ibid., 37.

3. "Presbyterians Do Mission in Partnership" (Louisville, Ky.: Presbyterian Church (U.S.A.), Worldwide Ministries Division, adopted by the 215th General Assembly, 2003). (See appendix C.)

4. Darrell L. Guder, *The Continuing Conversion of the Church* (Grand Rapids: Wm. B. Eerdmans Publishing Co., 2000), 73.

5. Joerg Rieger, *God and the Excluded: Visions and Blindspots in Contemporary Theology* (Minneapolis: Fortress Press, 2001), 105.

6. Ibid., 191.

CHAPTER 4: COMPASSION

1. Kristine A. Haig, *Presbyterians Today* (June 2002): 4.

2. *The Constitution of the Presbyterian Church (U.S.A.)*, Part II, *Book of Order* (Louisville, Ky.: Office of the General Assembly, 2001), W-7.3004.

3. Jon Sobrino, *The Principle of Mercy: Taking the Crucified People from the Cross* (Maryknoll, N.Y.: Orbis Books, 1994), 16.

4. Walter Brueggemann, *The Prophetic Imagination* (Philadelphia: Fortress Press, 1978), 85.

5. David Bosch, *Transforming Mission* (Maryknoll, N.Y.: Orbis Books, 1991), 290. For more about the prodigal and other images, please see Sherron George,"The Quest for Images of Missionaries in a 'Post-Missionary Era,'" *Missiology* 30, no. 1 (January 2002): 51–65.

6. Ofelia Ortega, "Mission as an Invitation for Life," *International Review of Mission* 88, nos. 348/349 (January/April 1999): 93.

7. Marian McClure, "Inside Harare—Compassion and Calling," *International Review of Mission* 88, nos. 348/349 (January/April 1999): 45, 47.

CHAPTER 5: HUMILITY

1. J. Andrew Kirk, *What Is Mission? Theological Explorations* (Minneapolis: Fortress Press, 2000), 188–91.

2. "Presbyterians Do Mission in Partnership" (Louisville, Ky.: Presbyterian Church (U.S.A.), Worldwide Ministries Division, adopted by the 215th General Assembly, 2003). (See appendix C.)

3. Fred B. Craddock, *Philippians* (Atlanta: John Knox Press, 1985), 38.

4. Claude E. Labrunie, "The Poor as Christ for the Rich," *Church & Society* (Sept/Oct 1993): 96.

5. Jürgen Moltmann, *The Trinity and the Kingdom,* trans. Margaret Kohl (Minneapolis: Fortress Press, 1993), 118–19.

6. "Partnership in Mission," Position Paper of the Commission on Ecumenical Mission and Relations of the United Presbyterian Church in the United States of America, approved March 17, 1964.

7. David J. Bosch, *Transforming Mission* (Maryknoll, N.Y.: Orbis Books, 1991), 291.

8. *Mission in the 1990s* (Louisville, Ky.: PC(USA) Worldwide Ministries Division, 1993), 4.

9. Bosch, *Transforming Mission,* 489.

10. Jean S. Stoner, ed., *Voices from Korea, U.S.A. and Brazil: The Reformed Faith and the Global Economy* (Louisville, Ky.: PC(USA) Office of Ecumenical Partnership, 2001), 20.

PART 3: WHAT? PRACTICES OF PARTNERSHIP

1. Craig Dykstra, "Reconceiving Practice," in *Shifting Boundaries: Contextual Approaches to the Structure of Theological Education,* ed. Barbara G. Wheeler and Edward Farley (Louisville, Ky.: Westminster/John Knox Press, 1991), 36, 37.

2. Dorothy C. Bass, ed., *Practicing Our Faith* (San Francisco: Jossey-Bass Publishers, 1997), xi.

3. "Presbyterians Do Mission in Partnership" (Louisville, Ky.: Presbyterian Church (U.S.A.), Worldwide Ministries Division, adopted by the 215th General Assembly, 2003). (See appendix C.)

4. Dykstra, "Reconceiving Practice," 44.

CHAPTER 6: OBSERVING AND PARTICIPATING

1. Anthony J. Gittins, *Ministry at the Margins* (Maryknoll, N.Y.: Orbis Books, 2002), 141.

2. "Presbyterians Do Mission in Partnership" (Louisville, Ky.: Presbyterian Church (U.S.A.), Worldwide Ministries Division, adopted by the 215th General Assembly, 2003). (See appendix C.)

3. J. Andrew Kirk, *What Is Mission?* (Minneapolis: Fortress Press, 2000), 191.

4. Frederick R. Wilson, ed., *The San Antonio Report: Your Will be Done: Mission in Christ's Way* (Geneva: WCC Publications, 1990), 37, 46.

5. Walter Brueggemann, *The Prophetic Imagination* (Philadelphia: Fortress Press, 1978), 88.

6. Rubem Alves, *Pai nosso: Meditações,* 6th ed. (São Paulo: Paulus, 1987), 57–62. Reprinted with permission.

CHAPTER 7: RECEIVING AND GIVING

1. Maya Angelou, *I Know Why The Caged Bird Sings* (New York: Bantam Books, 1993), 93, 100, 101.

2. Michael Downey, *Altogether Gift: A Trinitarian Spirituality* (Maryknoll, N.Y.: Orbis Books, 2000), 37.

3. Anthony Gittens, *Ministry at the Margins* (Maryknoll, N.Y.: Orbis Books, 2002), 118.

4. Jon Sobrino. *The Principle of Mercy: Taking the Crucified People from the Cross* (Maryknoll, N.Y.: Orbis Books, 1997), 154

5. Ibid., 159.

6. Downey, *Altogether Gift,* 66.

7. Darrell L. Guder, *The Continuing Conversion of the Church* (Grand Rapids: Wm. B. Eerdmans Publishing Co., 2000), 70.

8. Anthony J. Gittens, *Reading the Clouds* (Liguori, Mo.: Liguori, 1999), 86.

9. Ibid., 87.

10. *Gathering for God's Future: Witness, Discipleship, Community* (Louisville, Ky.: PC(USA) Worldwide Ministries Division, adopted by the 215th General Assembly, 2003), 2–5.

CHAPTER 8: SIGNS OF GOD'S TRANSFORMATION

1. Sherron George, "The Quest for Images of Missionaries in a 'Post-missionary Era,'" *Missiology* 30, no. 1 (January 2002): 54.

2. Vinay Samuel, "Mission as Transformation," in *Mission as Transformation,* ed. Vinay Samuel and Chris Sugden (Irvine, Calif.: Regnum, 1999), 231–32.

3. Ibid., 233.

4. Ross and Gloria Kinsler, *The Biblical Jubilee and the Struggle for Life* (Maryknoll, N.Y.: Orbis Books, 1999), 58.

5. Ibid., 128.
6. *The Constitution of the Presbyterian Church (U.S.A.),* Part II, *Book of Order* (Louisville, Ky.: Office of the General Assembly, 2001), G-30401d.
7. Philip L. Wickeri, *Partnership, Solidarity and Friendship: Transforming Structures in Mission* (Louisville, Ky.: Presbyterian Church (U.S.A.), Worldwide Ministries Division, 2003), 17–19.
8. *Book of Order,* G-3.0200.
9. Ibid., G-3.0300.
10. *Book of Order,* W-7.7001.
11. *Gathering for God's Future: Witness, Discipleship, Community* (Louisville, Ky.: Presbyterian Church (U.S.A.), Worldwide Ministries Division, adopted by the 215th General Assembly, 2003), 17.
12. Anthony J. Gittens, *Ministry at the Margins* (Maryknoll, N.Y.: Orbis Books, 2002), 8.

APPENDIX A: A GUIDE FOR GROUP REFLECTION AND PRACTICE

1. "Presbyterians Do Mission in Partnership" (Louisville, Ky.: Presbyterian Church (U.S.A.), Worldwide Ministries Division, adopted by the 215th General Assembly, 2003). (See appendix C.)
2. Ibid.

APPENDIX B: CASE STUDIES

1. Tom Montgomery-Fate, *Beyond the White Noise* (St. Louis: Chalice Press, 1997), 33, 34.
2. Ibid., 34.
3. Ibid., 41–42.
4. *Mission Yearbook for Prayer and Study* (Louisville, Ky.: Mission Interpretation and Promotion, Congregational Ministries Publishing, PC[USA], 2001), 255

APPENDIX C: "PRESBYTERIANS DO MISSION IN PARTNERSHIP"

1. This policy statement was produced by the Presbyterian Church (U.S.A.), Worldwide Ministries Division and adopted by the 215th General Assembly. Reprinted with permission.
2. In Latin, *Missio Dei*
3. *The Constitution of the Presbyterian Church (U.S.A.),* Part II, *Book of Order* (Louisville, Ky.: Office of the General Assembly, 2001), G-9.0103.
4. Ibid., G-3.0300.

Bibliography

"Accompaniment: The Missiological Vision." Part 1 in *Global Mission in the Twenty-first Century: A Vision of Evangelical Faithfulness in God's Mission.* Evangelical Lutheran Church in America, Division for Global Mission. Also available online at http://www.elca.org/dgm/policy/gm2/full.pdf.

Alves, Rubem. *Pai nosso: Meditações.* 6th ed. São Paulo: Paulus, 1987.

Arias, Mortimer. *Announcing the Reign of God.* Philadelphia: Fortress Press, 1984.

Arias, Mortimer and Alan Johnson. *The Great Commission: Biblical Models for Evangelism.* Nashville: Abingdon Press, 1992.

Bass, Dorothy C., ed. *Practicing Our Faith.* San Francisco: Jossey-Bass Publishers, 1997.

Boff, Leonardo. *A Trindade e a Sociedade.* 5th ed. Petropolis, RJ: Editora Vozes, 1999.

Bonk, Jonathan J. *Missions and Money.* Maryknoll, N.Y.: Orbis Books, 2000.

Bosch, David. *Transforming Mission.* Maryknoll, N.Y.: Orbis Books, 1991.

Brown, Raymond. *The Gospel according to John I–XII.* Anchor Bible, Vol. 29. New York: Doubleday, 1966.

Brown, Raymond. *The Gospel according to John XIII–XXI.* Anchor Bible, Vol. 29A. New York: Doubleday, 1970.

Brueggemann, Walter. *The Prophetic Imagination.* Philadelphia: Fortress Press, 1978.

Brueggemann, Walter. *Hope for the World: Mission in a Global Context.* Louisville, Ky.: Westminster John Knox Press, 2001.

A Celebration of Life: Gifts from Latin Americans. Louisville, Ky.: Presbyterian Church (U.S.A.), Congregational Ministries Division: Mission Interpretation and Promotion, 1996.

Comblin, José. *Sent from the Father: Meditations on the Fourth Gospel,* translated by Carl Kabat. Maryknoll, N.Y.: Orbis Books, 1979.

Congregations in Global Mission: Stepping into God's Future. A Conference Report. Louisville, Ky.: Presbyterian Church (U.S.A.), Worldwide Ministries Division, 2000.

The Constitution of the Presbyterian Church (U.S.A.), Part II, *Book of Order.* Louisville, Ky.: Office of the General Assembly, 2003.

Craddock, Fred B. *Luke: Interpretation.* Louisville, Ky.: Westminster/John Knox Press, 1990.

Craddock, Fred B. *Philippians: Interpretation.* Atlanta: John Knox Press, 1985.

Downey, Michael. *Altogether Gift: A Trinitarian Spirituality.* Maryknoll, N.Y.: Orbis Books, 2000.

Dykstra, Craig. "Reconceiving Practice." In *Shifting Boundaries: Contextual Approaches to the Structure of Theological Education.* Edited by Barbara G. Wheeler and Edward Farley. Louisville, Ky.: Westminster/John Knox Press, 1991.

Elizondo, Virgilio. *Galilean Journey.* Seventh printing. Maryknoll, N.Y.: Orbis Books, 1996.

Erdmann, Martin. "Mission in John's Gospel and Letters." In *Mission in the New Testament: An Evangelical Approach.* Edited by William J. Larkin Jr. and Joel F. Williams. Maryknoll, N.Y.: Orbis Books, 1998.

Escobar, Samuel. *Changing Tides: Latin America and World Mission Today.* Maryknoll, N.Y.: Orbis Books, 2002.

Freire, Paulo. *Pedagogia do Oprimido.* 13th edition. Rio de Janeiro: Paz e Terra, 1984.

Gathering for God's Future: Witness, Discipleship, Community. Louisville, Ky.: Presbyterian Church (U.S.A.), Worldwide Ministries Division, adopted by the 215th General Assembly, 2003.

George, Sherron K. *Meeting Your Neighbor: Multiculturalism in Luke and Acts* (Louisville, Ky.: Presbyterian Church (U.S.A.), 2000).

George, Sherron K. "The Mission of the Church." In *A Passion for the Gospel: Confessing Jesus Christ for the 21st Century.* Edited by Mark Achtemeier and Andrew Purves. Louisville, Ky.: Geneva Press, 2000.

George, Sherron K. "Local-Global Mission: The Cutting Edge." *Missiology* 28, no. 2 (2000): 187–97.

George, Sherron K. "The Quest for Images of Missionaries in a 'Post-missionary Era.'" *Missiology* 30, no. 1 (2002): 51–65.

Gittins, Anthony J. *Gifts and Strangers.* Mahwah, N.J.: Paulist Press, 1989.

Gittins, Anthony J. *Bread for the Journey.* Maryknoll, N.Y.: Orbis Books, 1993.

Gittens. Anthony J. *Reading the Clouds.* Liguori, Mo.: Liguori, 1999.

Gittins, Anthony J. *Ministry at the Margins.* Maryknoll, N.Y.: Orbis Books, 2002.

Guder, Darrell L., ed. *Missional Church.* Grand Rapids: Wm. B. Eerdmans Publishing Co., 1998.

Guder, Darrell L. *The Continuing Conversion of the Church.* Grand Rapids: Wm. B. Eerdmans Publishing Co., 2000.

Gundry-Volf, Judith M. and Miroslav Volf. *A Spacious Heart: Essays on Identity and Belonging.* Christian Mission and Modern Culture series. Harrisburg, Pa.: Trinity Press International, 1997.

Guthrie, Shirley C. *God for the World–Church for the World: The Mission of the Church in Today's World.* Louisville, Ky.: Witherspoon Press, 2000.

Gutiérrez, Gustavo. *The God of Life.* Translated by Matthew J. O'Connell. Maryknoll, N.Y.: Orbis Books, 1998.

Herzog, William R. *Parables as Subversive Speech: Jesus as Pedagogue of the Oppressed.* Louisville, Ky.: Westminster John Knox Press, 1994.

John, Thomas. *A Strange Accent: the Reflections of a Missionary to the United States.* Louisville, Ky.: Worldwide Ministries Division, 1996.

Kinsler, Ross and Gloria Kinsler. *The Biblical Jubilee and the Struggle for Life.* Maryknoll, N.Y.: Orbis Books, 1999.

Kirk, J. Andrew. *What Is Mission? Theological Explorations.* Minneapolis: Fortress Press, 2000.

Köstenberger, Andreas J. *The Missions of Jesus & The Disciples according to the Fourth Gospel.* Grand Rapids: Wm. B. Eerdmans Publishing Co., 1998.

Labrunie, Claude E. "The Poor as Christ for the Rich." *Church & Society* (Sept/Oct 1993): 94–96.

Law, Eric H. F. *The Wolf Shall Dwell with the Lamb: A Spirituality for Leadership in a Multicultural Community.* St. Louis: Chalice Press, 1993.

Lee, Jung Young. *Marginality: The Key to Multicultural Theology.* Minneapolis: Fortress Press, 1995.

Legrand, Lucien."The Gospel of John as a Missionary Synthesis." *Unity and Plurality: Mission in the Bible.* Translated by Robert R. Barr. Maryknoll, N.Y.: Orbis Books, 1990.

Lloyd-Sidle and Bonnie Sue Lewis, eds. *Teaching Mission in a Global Context.* Louisville, Ky.: Geneva Press, 2001.

Martin, Ralph P. *The New Century Bible Commentary Philippians.* Grand Rapids: Wm. B. Eerdmans Publishing Co., 1980.

McClure, Marian. "Inside Harare—Compassion and Calling." *International Review of Mission* 88, nos. 348/349 (1999): 45–50.

Mission in the 1990s. Louisville, Ky.: Presbyterian Church (U.S.A.), Worldwide Ministries Division, adopted by the 205th General Assembly, 1993.

Moltmann, Jürgen. *The Trinity and the Kingdom.* Minneapolis: Fortress Press, 1993.

Montgomery-Fate, Tom. *Beyond the White Noise.* St. Louis: Chalice Press, 1997.

Newbigin, Lesslie. *The Light Has Come.* Grand Rapids: Wm. B. Eerdmans Publishing Co., 1982.

Ortega, Ofelia. "Mission as an Invitation for Life." *International Review of Mission* 88, nos. 348/349 (1999): 88–96.

"Partnership in Mission." Position Paper of the Commission on Ecumenical Mission and Relations of the United Presbyterian Church in the United States of America, approved March 17, 1964.

Pohl, Christine D. *Making Room: Recovering Hospitality as a Christian Tradition.* Grand Rapids: Wm. B. Eerdmans Publishing Co., 1999.

Rhodes, Stephen A. *Where the Nations Meet.* Downers Grove, Ill.: Intervarsity Press, 1998.

Rieger, Joerg. *God and the Excluded: Visions and Blindspots in Contemporary Theology.* Minneapolis: Fortress Press, 2001.

Samuel, Vinay and Chris Sugden, eds. *Mission as Transformation.* Irvine, Calif.: Regnum, 1999.

Schreiter, Robert J. *The New Catholicity: Theology between the Global and the Local.* Maryknoll, N.Y.: Orbis Books, 1997.

Shenk, Wilbert R. *Changing Frontiers of Mission.* Maryknoll, N.Y.: Orbis Books, 1999.

Sobrino, Jon. *The Principle of Mercy: Taking the Crucified People from the Cross.* Maryknoll, N.Y.: Orbis Books, 1997.

Stackhouse, Max L., Tim Dearborn, and Scott Paeth, eds. *The Local Church in a Global Era: Reflection for a New Century.* Grand Rapids: Wm. B. Eerdmans Publishing Co., 2000.

Stoner, Jean S., ed. *Voices from Korea, U.S.A. and Brazil: The Reformed Faith and the Global Economy.* Louisville, Ky.: Presbyterian Church (U.S.A.), Office of Ecumenical Partnership, 2001.

Stroupe, Nibs and Inez Fleming. *While We Run This Race.* Maryknoll, N.Y.: Orbis Books, 1995.

Turn To The Living God: A Call to Evangelism in Jesus Christ's Way. Louisville, Ky.: Presbyterian Church (U.S.A.), Office of the General Assembly, 1991.

Warkentin, Raija. "Begging as Resistance: Wealth and Christian Missionaries in Postcolonial Zaire." *Missiology: An International Review* 29, no. 2 (2001): 143–63.

Wickeri, Philip L. *Partnership, Solidarity and Friendship: Transforming Structures in Mission.* Louisville, Ky.: Presbyterian Church (U.S.A.), Worldwide Ministries Division, 2003.

Wilson, Frederick R., ed. *The San Antonio Report: Your Will be Done: Mission in Christ's Way.* Geneva: WCC Publications, 1990.

LaVergne, TN USA
12 January 2010
169690LV00005B/1/A